COOPERATIVE LEARNING IN THE ELEMENTARY CLASSROOM

Lawrence Lyman
Harvey C. Foyle
Tara S. Azwell

Developments in Classroom Instruction Series
An NEA Professional Library Publication

The authors would like to thank the following persons for sharing their expertise in this work: Ed Abbuehl (Eisenhower Middle School, Topeka, Kansas), Margaret Davidson (Butcher Children's School, Emporia, Kansas), Denny Dey (Benedictine College, Atchison, Kansas), Gwen Eidman (Cotton-wood Falls Grade School, Cottonwood Falls, Kansas), Joanne Foyle (William Allen White Elementary School, Emporia, Kansas), Darcy Kraus (Whitson Elementary School, Topeka, Kansas), and Jerry Long (Emporia State University, Emporia, Kansas).

Note

Library of Congress Cataloging-in-Publication Data
Lyman, Lawrence.
    Cooperative learning in the elementary classroom / Lawrence Lyman, Harvey C. Foyle, Tara S. Azwell.
    p. cm. — (Developments in classroom instruction series)
Includes bibliographical references (p.).
ISBN 0-8106-3042-7 1. Group work in education. 2. Education, Elementary—United States. 3. Team learning approach in education. 4. Classroom management—United States. I. Foyle, Harvey Charles. II. Azwell, Tara S. III. Title. IV. Series.
LB1032.L96 1993   934125
371.2'5'0973—dc20   CIP

CONTENTS

PREFACE

Elementary school educators face specific challenges as they strive to meet the academic and social needs of their students. This book addresses a broad audience of elementary educators who have already had some contact with cooperative learning as a resource for innovative learning in their classrooms. These readers can be divided into two more specific audiences.

The first audience includes educators who have heard about and want to try cooperative learning but who have had little opportunity to do so. For these educators, the authors have tried to provide background on cooperative learning and specific ideas for getting started successfully. The beginner will also want to refer to the Selected References listed at the end of each chapter and the bibliography at the end of the book for a more thorough understanding of cooperative learning. Many helpful tips are given in the Postscript, 'Initial Use of Cooperative Learning,' which follows Chapter 11.

The second audience for this book consists of those educators who have already had some experience with cooperative learning. For these readers, the authors have made connections between cooperative learning and other important educational topics—whole language, critical thinking, curriculum integration, and so on. We hope these connections will expand the reader's view of cooperative learning and stimulate creative adaptations of the material in this book.

Our work with elementary students and educators has convinced us that cooperative learning should be a part of the instructional program in every classroom in the intermediate elementary grades. We hope this work provides practicing educators with strategies for the successful implementation of this important teaching methodology.

—Lawrence Lyman
Harvey C. Foyle
Tara S. Azwell

Chapter 1

COOPERATIVE LEARNING COMPONENTS AND THE LEARNING NEEDS OF ELEMENTARY STUDENTS

A child in itself is not an imperfect creature, he is not a half-ready adult, but he is an independent individual. So a tadpole is satisfied with itself, its operation is as perfect as that of a frog and it is not an imperfect, insufficiently functioning frog! . . . If a child is an independent creature with a whole life, an individual with specific needs, then we can draw the conclusion that education, from the child's point, is not preparation for life but it is life itself.

—Claparede

Teachers of elementary students are faced with unprecedented challenges as they strive for excellence in the classroom. By the time children have moved through the primary grades, they have too often become "sorted" into distinct groups of "winners" and "losers" in the critical areas of academic achievement and social interactions. Some students are successful both academically and socially, while some succeed in one of the two areas. Some students are unsuccessful both in learning performance and in getting along with their peers.

The teacher is also confronted with rising expectations for student performance. Administrators and parents often demand increased teacher accountability for student-learning performance. Fiscal resources too often lag behind the demands for excellence, while class size continues to increase in many areas. School populations are becoming more ethnically and economically diverse, which can cause increased tension among students.

Educators are responding to these challenges with promising innovations such as Total Quality Management (Glasser 1990, Bonstingl 1991) adapted from the business sector and Outcomes-Based Edu-

9

cation (Kansas 1991), which seek to restructure the relationships between school personnel, students, parents, and the community. Mastery learning (Guskey 1985) suggests that all students can achieve reasonable levels of success on critical skills identified by the school when given sufficient time and motivation. Curricular innovations such as whole language and curriculum integration (Jacobs 1989) suggest that learning can be made more relevant to student needs and interests and that students can become more active learners.

Critical to the success of these innovations is a classroom-management structure that facilitates group cooperation and motivates students to put forth effort to learn (Foyle and Lyman 1991). Cooperative learning is a methodology that is proving effective in many elementary classrooms in helping to encourage productive student interaction and behavior. No teacher alone, however skilled and dedicated, can meet the needs of the increasingly diverse student population entering the upper elementary grades each year. Students must become actively involved in helping to improve their own schooling.

To make this contribution, the elementary school child needs to appreciate the diversity of other children and to develop social interaction skills that will foster positive relationships with them. The elementary school child also needs to develop the individual skills and motivation that increase success in school settings. Cooperative learning is an instructional methodology that meets both these needs in the classroom.

Cooperative learning involves students in small group classroom learning activities (Foyle and Lyman 1991). It is based upon the research of social psychology, the experiences of educators in small group teaching, and the observations of experts in the area of group dynamics. Studies find that cooperative learning increases academic achievement and student interaction while being easy to use and cost effective. Other benefits of cooperative learning include improved student behavior, more positive student attitudes toward the class, and better attendance (Slavin 1990).

Cooperative learning holds particular promise for elementary teachers. It increases individual student motivation, encourages inter-

FIGURE 1.1
COOPERATIVE LEARNING COMPONENTS AND LEARNING NEEDS

HETEROGENEOUS GROUPS "max mix"	Sense of identity Sense of acceptance/inclusion Sense of belonging to a group
POSITIVE INTERDEPENDENCE "pulling together"	Trust building Child-directed Motivation Learner responsibility
GROUP INTERACTION "Let's do it!"	Communication skills Social skills Problem solving/conflict resolution Active involvement
GROUP REWARD "We did it!"	Task completion/pride Bonding to a group Motivation
INDIVIDUAL ACCOUNTABILITY "I did my part."	Value to group/belonging Learner responsibility Individual progress check
SUCCESS "We did it well!"	Group processing/evaluation Planning/self-direction Motivation

active group processes, and rewards successful group participation. In fact, cooperative learning is philosophically more attuned to the instruction of students than traditional methods. Many educators still treat elementary students as the *tabla rosa,* the blank slate, or empty bin, ready to be filled with facts and figures. Educators who use cooperative learning are more philosophically in agreement with the concept that children's growth and learning are a continuous process rather than a product that is finished at any given moment.

A VARIETY OF METHODS

A variety of cooperative learning methods has developed since the early 1970s. Some methods are complex while other methods are fairly simple. Cooperative learning groups, when observed in the classroom setting, appear similar to small groups in general. Cooperative learning groups, however, are distinguished by the components found in Figure 1.1, Cooperative Learning Components and Learning Needs, (Foyle, Lyman, and Thies 1991; Lyman and Foyle 1990). Each particular strategy's proponent has specifically written and explained his or her ideas. The following table summarizes cooperative learning strategies from which an elementary educator may choose.

SUMMARY OF COOPERATIVE LEARNING STRATEGIES

Type	Author	Applicable Grades	Group Size
STAD*	Slavin	2-8	
TGT**	Slavin	4-12	3-4
Jigsaw	Slavin	4-Adult	3-4
Think-Pair-Share (TPS)	Frank Lyman	Pre-Adult	2
Simple Structures	Kagan	Pre-Adult	2-5
Learning Together	Johnsons	K-Adult	3-4
Group Investigation	Sharans	4-Adult	2-6

*Student Teams Achievement Divisions
**Teams, Games, Tournaments

STAD (Slavin 1991) is one of the easier strategies to use because subject content can be presented in the traditional way. Individual student assessment can use the teacher's traditional criteria and methods. After the teacher presents the lesson, student teams work on assignments cooperatively in order to master the subject's material. In studies conducted by Newmann and Thompson (1987), STAD was the most successful of the cooperative learning techniques studied when compared with traditional teaching methods.

TGT (Slavin 1991) is similar to STAD but with the addition of a competitive tournament. After studying the material with team members, students compete with other students of similar achievement levels to win points for their teams. Individual student assessment is then conducted.

Jigsaw II (Slavin 1991) places students in groups to read parts of a chapter, article, or text or to read different materials dealing with a similar topic. The students meet to review their readings. Then student groups are reformed so that original team members are divided among "expert" groups with other students from other teams who have read the same material. After discussion within the "expert" group, students return to their original teams to further discuss the material. Questions about the material can be provided to the original teams and/or the "expert" groups. Assessment of learning is done by test or quiz on an individual basis to insure individual accountability.

Learning Together is a strategy promoted by Johnson and Johnson (1991). Students are given cooperative tasks that are intended to create positive interdependence and encourage group interaction. Rewards may be provided for both individual and group performance.

Group Investigation (Sharan and Sharan 1992) requires that students work together to decide what information is needed, how the information will be organized, and how the information will be presented. In organizing the tasks and facilitating the group work, teachers encourage students to develop the skills of applying information, synthesizing information, and inferring from information related to the subject being studied.

Spencer Kagan (1990) has developed and promotes a wide range of simple cooperative learning structures. One such simple structure is Roundtable. It can be used for group building, reviewing information, practicing skills, and brainstorming. Students are grouped in heterogeneous teams of three or four. Each team has a single sheet of paper and one pencil or pen. The teacher asks a question that has many possible correct answers. Each student contributes one possible correct answer and passes the paper clockwise to another student in the group. After time is called, teams with the most correct answers are recognized. Each team then discusses its work and identifies possible ways to improve. A variation has each student in the team start a piece of paper by writing an answer and passing it on so that several papers are circulating at the same time.

Frank Lyman (1993) of the University of Maryland has developed Think-Pair-Share (TPS). TPS can improve student participation and interest in class discussions. Because the strategy is easily implemented, it provides a successful first experience in cooperative learning for elementary school students. In TPS, students listen while the teacher poses a question or problem related to the learning objective. The students try to come up with possible answers individually. After students have had the opportunity to consider the question or problem individually, they are paired with another student to discuss or work on their responses. The teacher obtains responses from the paired discussion groups. TPS allows each student to become actively involved in learning by sharing ideas with at least one other student. TPS is supported by research on wait-time and cuing.

Other cooperative learning strategies include Kagan's Numbered Heads Together, Co-op Co-op, Simple Structures (Kagan 1990), and Tribes (Gibbs 1987).

Regardless of which strategy is chosen, cooperative learning brings together the cognitive domain (knowledge) and the affective domain (feelings) within groups of interacting students. The cognitive question, "Do I have the necessary information?" is balanced with the affective question, "Have I listened to the information?" In the interactive setting of the cooperative small group, the question becomes,

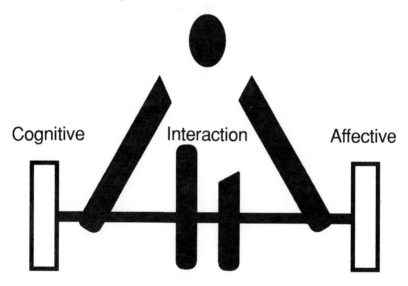

Figure 1.2
Cooperative Learning Unites
Cognitive and Affective Domains

Cognitive

Do I have the necessary information?

Does it apply to me?

How does it fit together?

How could I use it in new and creative ways?

What is the value of this information?

Interaction

Have I had the opportunity to discuss my reactions to this information with others?

Have I refined, expanded, and increased my understanding of the information by discussing it with others?

Affective

Have I listened to the information?

How do I feel about the information?

Will I use this information?

"Have I had the opportunity to discuss my reactions to this information with others?" (see Figure 1.2).

SELECTED REFERENCES

Bonstingl, J. J. 1991. "Total Quality in Education: A Prescription for Improving Our Schools." *The Early Adolescence Magazine* 5(6), 2×6.

Foyle, H. C., and Lyman, L. 1991. *Cooperative Learning: What You Need to Know.* (Pamphlet for parents.) Washington, D.C.: National Education Association.

_____ 1993. *The Interactive Classroom.* (Videotape set: Part 1A Cooperative learning: Overview; Part 2–Cooperative learning: A step-by-step approach.) Washington, D.C.: National Education Association.

Foyle, H. C., Lyman, L., and Alexander Thies, S. 1991. *Cooperative Learning in the Early Childhood Classroom.* Washington, D.C.: National Education Association.

Gibbs, J. 1987. *TRIBES: A Process for Social Development and Cooperative Learning.* Santa Rosa, Calif.: Center Source Publications.

Glasser, W. 1990. *The Quality School: Managing Students Without Coercion.* New York: Harper and Row, Publishers.

Guskey, T. R. 1985. *Implementing Mastery Learning.* Belmont, Calif.: Wadsworth Publishing Company.

Jacobs, H. H. (ed). 1989. *Interdisciplinary Curriculum: Design and Implementation.* Alexandria, Va.: Association for Supervision and Curriculum Development.

Johnson, D. W., and Johnson, R. T. 1991. *Learning Together and Alone: Cooperative, Competitive, and Individualistic Learning,* 3rd edition. Englewood Cliffs, N.J.: Prentice-Hall.

Kagan, S. 1990. *Cooperative Learning Resources for Teachers.* San Juan Capistrano, Calif.: Resources for Teachers.

Kansas State Board of Education. 1991. *Kansas Quality Performance Accreditation: A Plan for Living, Learning, and Working in a Global Society.* Topeka, Kans.: Kansas State Board of Education.

Lyman, F. 1993. *Think-Pair-Share.* (Videotape). Washington, D.C.: National Education Association.

Lyman, L., and Foyle, H.C. 1990. *Cooperative Grouping for Interactive Learning: Students, Teachers, and Administrators.* Washington, D.C.: National Education Association.

Newmann, F. M., and Thompson, J. A. 1987. *Effects of Cooperative Learning on Achievement in Secondary Schools: A Summary of Research.* Madison, Wis.: Wisconsin Center for Education Research, University of Wisconsin-Madison.

Sharan, Y., and Sharan, S. 1992. *Expanding Cooperative Learning Through Group Investigation.* New York: Teachers College Press.

Slavin, R. E. 1990. *Cooperative Learning: Theory, Research, and Practice.* Englewood Cliffs, N.J.: Prentice Hall.

Slavin, R. E. 1991. *Using Student Team Learning,* 3rd edition. Baltimore, Md.: The Johns Hopkins Team Learning Project, Center for Research on Elementary and Middle Schools, Johns Hopkins University.

Chapter 2

RESTRUCTURING THE CLASSROOM FOR COOPERATION

It is good to rub and polish our brains against those of others.

— Montaigne

Many elementary students are accustomed to working individually or competitively in school. They view classmates as adversaries, competing for teacher and peer approval. In some classrooms students guard their work from others, viewing the sharing of ideas as "cheating." Changing from such orientations to a classroom structure that encourages cooperation requires careful planning on the part of the classroom teacher.

Even if students have had previous experience with cooperative learning in primary grades, each school year provides a different set of peers and differing teacher expectations. Some students have already begun to feel that they are academic or social failures in school. More talented peers may reinforce this image and be reluctant to work with the "losers."

From the first day of school, the teacher must work to change the structure of the classroom. Students must be encouraged to work together, to support other students, and to interact socially with students who are different in personality, cultural background, gender, and ethnicity.

This process must begin from the very start of the year because students will become increasingly resistant to cooperation as the school year progresses. In order to successfully restructure the classroom, the teacher must begin with a promise to students and follow by engaging them in group-building activities that help the teacher assess what further group skills they will need.

BEGIN WITH A PROMISE

To students who have experienced academic or social failure in school, the prospect of another school year of continued failure and humiliation is discouraging. While all elementary students need to begin a new school year on a positive note, it is absolutely vital that students who have experienced failure in school begin to believe that they can be successful in a new and different classroom environment.

The teacher can create a feeling of hope for all students by making a promise to students that this year can be successful for them. Such a promise states the need for students to make an effort to learn and get along with others. The teacher also points out that all students have something to contribute to the classroom and need to take an active part in class activities. An example of such a promise follows.

A PROMISE TO MY STUDENTS

When you come into this class, you can be sure that you can be successful if you do your best. I'm glad to be your teacher, and I am happy you are my student.

When you come into this class, you have a group of classmates who can become your friends. Your fellow students will work with you and help you in this class. We care about each other.

When you come into this class, you bring talents, skills, and ideas that can make our classroom a better place. You can count on us to work with you. I know you care about us.

If you work hard, this will be the best year you have ever had in school. Let's work, play, laugh, and share together.

By affirming the potential for a successful year, the teacher makes the first important step toward creating the environment for successful cooperative learning.

GROUP BUILDING

Once the commitment to developing a cooperative environment is made to students, the teacher needs to promote successful interaction among students through structured group-building activities. Group-building activities help students to get to know one another through positive, successful experiences. Also, observing student interaction during group-building activities provides the teacher with important information about individuals that is useful in making grouping decisions and in identifying needed social skills.

According to Lyman and Foyle (1990), groups should have five key components:

- *Heterogeneous Grouping:* Students should have the opportunity to work with every other student in class during the first week of school in at least one type of group-building activity.

- *Positive Interdependence:* The activities should be structured so that students are actively involved in the activity and believe that their participation is needed for the group to be successful. Successful group-building activities discourage one student from doing all the work by assigning specific responsibilities to each individual.

- *Individual Accountability:* All students must be accountable for working on the task. To ensure individual accountability during group-building activities, the teacher will actively monitor the group work, encouraging reluctant students to participate. Students can also be taught to encourage their peers to participate and to praise them when they do participate. The teacher may wish to place reluctant students with more socially successful peers who can provide such encouragement.

- *Group Reward:* Group-building activities are usually fun for students, and the enjoyment of participating is often a reward in itself. The teacher may also choose to praise group efforts, give a small food reward, allow extra recess time, or display group products as rewards for successful participation in group building. All groups must be able to earn the reward offered, or hard feelings can emerge that impede the group-building process.

- *Success:* Group-building activities need to be designed so that students feel successful in their initial efforts to cooperate. Grading of group-building activities is almost always inappropriate, although some teachers encourage students at the end of the first week of school by telling them that everyone in class has an "A" for the week. The remainder of the school year provides ample time to grade students on more exact criteria.

There are three basic types of group-building structures that work well with elementary school students. Students can be given a *whole group task,* which encourages awareness of other students. *Pairing students* may be necessary at first with groups that have had little previous experience with cooperative learning. *Activities for groups of three, four, or five students* can be introduced when students have been successful in paired group-building activities.

Whole Group Tasks

The whole group task is designed to help students become aware of the other students in the classroom. Students may be given a worksheet with information about other students, or the teacher may lead a memory game in which students try to recall facts about their new classmates. In the following task, students begin to interact with other students by obtaining classmates' signatures during a class "scavenger hunt."

ACTIVITY—SIGNATURE SCAVENGERS

Objective:	Students will learn about each other by obtaining classmates' signatures on an information sheet.
Procedure:	Each student is given a sheet (see Activity Sheet Appendix, Figures 2.1 and 2.2) with information that he or she is to discover by visiting with other students. Before beginning, allow students to look over their sheets and ask questions if they do

not understand any of the items. A classmate's signature can be used only one time per sheet. The student may sign his or her own sheet once if appropriate. Provide a time limit of five minutes and give the following guidelines: no running, no pushing, no loud talking.

Follow-Up: Each student thinks of an item to be added to a future scavenger sheet. These items are compiled into sheets, and the class uses one sheet per day until all items have been shared.

Paired Group-Building Task

Student cooperation begins in pairs. In a classroom of students who have had limited experience in cooperation, the teacher may decide to have each student work with every other student in class during the first weeks of school. When students are reluctant to work with other students, the teacher can remind the students that the activity will be a short one and that the teacher has confidence that the students can work together well. A simple pairing activity may involve students in solving a puzzle, recalling information, or matching ideas. In the following activity, students are asked to recall metaphorical creatures.

ACTIVITY—CREATURE FEATURE

Objective: Working in pairs, students will identify creatures missing from familiar metaphors.

Procedure: Students are given a worksheet (see Activity Sheet Appendix, Figure 2.3) with metaphors that contain the names of birds, insects, fish, or other animals. Students help each other name the correct creatures. Students should be instructed to do the ones that are easy for them and then go back and try the rest. Students should take turns recording the answers the pair comes up with. Assure students that spelling does not count and that some items may have more than one correct answer.

Answers: (1) cat, (2) swan, (3) mule, (4) pig, (5) duck, (6) lamb, (7) hog, (8) cow, (9) elephant, (10) leopard, (11) bear or bull, (12) hare, (13) frog, (14) lion and lamb, (15) cats and dogs, (16)

23

dog, (17) bull, (18) horse, (19) wolf, (20) goat, (21) butterfly and bee, (22) crocodile, (23) monkey, (24) cat, (25) goose and gander, (26) fly, (27) chicken,

Follow-Up: Student pairs think of another metaphor involving a bird, an insect, a fish, or another type of animal or make up a new one of their own. Each pair shares its idea with the other class members who try to guess the creature.

When pairs are used in group-building activities, they can easily be combined into groups of four for extension of the activity or follow-up. The following activity begins with pairs and the pairs can later work with other pairs in groups of four.

ACTIVITY—MATCHING GAME

Objective: Students will find as many matches as possible in a designated time period.

Procedure: The teacher puts students in pairs. Each pair is given a copy of the items (see Activity Sheet Appendix, Figure 2.4) and is instructed to find as many matches as possible in the time designated (10 minutes is enough). A match is made if both students discover, for example, that they like chocolate ice cream (item 1).

Follow-Up: Two pairs come together for another round of the activity. Students may use ideas they originally came up with in their pairs, or may need to find different ideas every group member can agree on. Items from this activity can provide a good lead-in for class discussion of standards for getting along with each other. For example, the teacher can ask groups to share their response to "something we expect of a friend" or "something we'd like to see more of." Responses can be displayed to remind students of ways to work cooperatively together.

Group-Building Activities for Groups of Three, Four, or Five

As students demonstrate that they can work cooperatively in pairs, the teacher can introduce group-building activities for groups of three, four, or five students. Caution should be exercised when students are in groups of three, as one student could be excluded by a pair of students in the group. In the following group-building activity, students learn more about each other by participating in a classroom poll.

ACTIVITY—CLASSROOM POLL

Objective: In groups, students will make a graph to display class responses to a poll.

Procedure: Each student is given a poll sheet (see Activity Sheet Appendix, Figure 2.5) to fill out individually. The student cuts out each of his or her answers on the lines indicated. This will provide eight pieces of data from each student in the class, so as many as eight groups of three or four students may be used. The teacher collects all answers for each question and clips the responses together (all brother and sister responses are clipped together, for example).

Students are grouped in heterogeneous groups of three or four. Each group is given all the responses to one of the poll items. The group works together to construct a bar graph of the data and shares its graph with the class. To make sure everyone does part of the task, the teacher may choose to assign roles such as "data reader," "grapher," "labeler," and "sharer."

Follow-Up: The teacher can ask group members to discuss what they did well in working together and share one idea with the class. Each group could also be asked to suggest a question for a future poll.

Teachers can find many sources for group-building activities. Ideas from professional magazines can be adapted to promote cooperation. Commercial games can be adapted to teach cooperation among students. For those who want more group builders and group-building resources, see the National Education Association book, *Cooperative Grouping for Interactive Learning: Students, Teachers, and Administrators* (Lyman and Foyle 1990). In the following group-building activity, fonts from the Macintosh computer program *MacWrite II* were used to create a code for students to solve in groups.

ACTIVITY—COMMUNICATION GROUP-BUILDER

Objective: Students will work in groups of three or four to decode a pictograph message.

Procedure: Students are grouped in heterogeneous groups of three or four students. Each group is given a copy of a pictograph and asked to work together to decode the message. For groups having difficulty, the teacher may want to tell the group that the "hint" pictures correspond to letters of the alphabet.

Follow-Up: Each group can design its own symbols and message for another group to decode.

Observing and Assessing: While students work together on group-building activities, the teacher gets to know the new class and assesses its cooperation skills. (See Activity Sheet Appendix, Figure 2.6 for some things to look for.)

On the basis of these observations, the teacher plans for successful implementation of cooperative learning in specific academic subject areas. For example, students who do not get along would usually not be grouped together. Care would be taken to make sure leaders are distributed throughout the groups to provide support for weaker students. The teacher will answer questions the students may have about grading and other issues.

CONCLUSION

The success of cooperative learning depends on how well the students have been prepared to work together in groups. Discouraged students who have experienced failure in school need reassurance that cooperative learning offers them a chance for success, while successful students need to know that cooperative learning does not threaten their success. Group-building activities provide each student with the opportunity to experience success while cooperating with others. The teacher is provided with the chance to make necessary student assessments which will be invaluable in structuring successful cooperative learning activities throughout the school year.

SELECTED REFERENCES

Gibbs, J. 1987. *Tribes: A Process for Social Development and Cooperative Learning*. Santa Rosa, Calif.: Center Source Publications.

Glasser, W. 1987. *Control Theory in the Classroom*. New York: Harper and Row.

Lyman, L., and Foyle, H. C. 1990. *Cooperative Grouping for Interactive Learning: Students, Teachers, and Administrators*. Washington, D.C.: National Education Association.

Rhoades, J., and McCabe, M. 1992. *The Cooperative Classroom: Social and Academic Activities*. Bloomington, Ind.: National Educational Service.

Chapter 3

PLANNING FOR AN INTERACTIVE CLASSROOM: THE STEP-BY-STEP PROCESS

You can do no harm to your students by encouraging their mutual cooperation.

—Foyle and Lyman

The benefits of cooperative learning are clear. But the steps to *implementing* cooperative learning must be spelled out so that teachers may move gradually from a traditional to a cooperative lesson design. After establishing a cooperative classroom environment, the elementary teacher plans to implement the subject matter that is usually taught. This is achieved through a step-by-step process that facilitates a broader climate of interactive learning among students. These steps are slightly different from the procedures that many teachers use in planning their units or lessons. As do all teaching strategies, cooperative learning requires a degree of caution when it is new and different for teacher and students (see the section in this chapter entitled Before You Implement Cooperative Learning).

BEFORE YOU IMPLEMENT COOPERATIVE LEARNING

The authors believe that no harm can come to students through the appropriate implementation of cooperative learning methods. However, cooperative learning can create questions and anxiety in students, parents, administrators, and colleagues. The following guidelines can help to minimize any negative effects that might come with implementing a new procedure.

1. *Start slowly.* Use cooperative learning sparingly until you are sure that what you are doing is benefiting your class.

2. *Avoid group grading.* Group grading can alarm parents of high achievers. Group grading is only for skilled practitioners of cooperative learning, and then only when adequate parent and administrator information has been provided in advance.
3. *Build an atmosphere that encourages cooperative learning.* Building student ownership, active participation, high expectations, and positive feelings creates a foundation for cooperative learning and for successful classroom management.
4. *Promote student success.* Early experiences with cooperative learning should be highly successful and rewarding for students.
5. *Tell administrators you are using cooperative learning methods.* Be ready to explain your goals, expected outcomes, and the benefits research associates with cooperative learning.
6. *Use other techniques and strategies as well as cooperative learning.* No technique is effective when used all the time.
7. *Monitor student reactions and conduct individual conferences with students.* This helps reassure those who are troubled by cooperative learning.
8. *Teach group processes to students.* Don't expect your students to already have the skills needed to work successfully in groups.
9. *Monitor the effectiveness of your teaching.* Use the same individual evaluation procedures you usually use. You may also wish to monitor student achievement; attitude; attendance; discipline referrals; and behavior in the playground, hallway, and lunchroom as indicators of the success of your methods.
10. *Network with other teachers.* A support group of other teachers who use cooperative learning is necessary for problem solving, celebration, and exchange of ideas.

STEP 1: CHOOSE YOUR CONTENT

In Step 1, the teacher identifies the appropriate content for a lesson that uses the cooperative learning approach. Criteria for student mastery are determined in advance. Various decisions are made by the teacher, such as how to initially present the material to the students.

A cooperative learning strategy is chosen based on the specific objectives, student population, and grade level identified by the teacher. Throughout this chapter the step-by-step process will be illustrated by using a class constitution unit.

Example:

Grade Level: Fourth through sixth grades
Topic: Social studies and language arts (creating a constitution in a classroom managed by cooperative learning methodology)
Objective: Students will cooperatively develop a constitution for students in the classroom.

STEP 2: ASSIGN HETEROGENEOUS GROUPS

In Step 2, the teacher groups the students prior to the class activity. Cooperative learning is usually best accomplished in heterogeneous groupings of students. Ethnic, racial, religious, gender, academic achievement, skill ability, and other factors may be used to group students. Mixed groups have the greatest potential for success in cooperative learning because student differences make for greater student interaction within the groups. Depending upon the cooperative learning strategy, students may be assigned to groups prior to the lesson or at the beginning of the lesson during class.

Example:

Group Size: Three students (not all of the same sex) per group

STEP 3: TEACH GROUP ROLES

In Step 3, the teacher instructs the students about the roles, if any, that are necessary for the cooperative learning lesson. There are a variety of roles that teachers can choose—facilitator, encourager, marker, writer, or observer. The number and functions of the student roles will vary according to the needs of the group, requirements of the task, and the time available. These group roles are actively taught or reviewed by the teacher so that the groups run smoothly.

Example:

Student Roles: 1. Reader: reads questions to the group
2. Recorder: records the group's responses
3. Encourager: assures that each student participates

STEP 4: ASSIGN THE TASK

In Step 4, the teacher chooses a task for the students to accomplish. The task may be one of process and/or of product. The task may facilitate creative thinking through brainstorming techniques or critical thinking through problem-solving techniques. The teacher states clearly the expectations for student learning and the purpose of the task. A time line for the activities is made clear to the students.

Example:

Classroom Rules: In many fourth through sixth grade classes, students have trouble getting along with one another. Usually, the classroom teacher dictates and enforces class rules. This cooperative learning lesson allows students to set classroom rules and support the teacher in enforcing them. The questions are stated in the vocabulary of fourth through sixth graders.
Time Involved: Four to five class sessions

STEP 5: MOVE INTO GROUPS

In Step 5, the students move into their group assignments. This usually involves pushing desks closer, resulting in some noise and confusion. At first, plan for desks to be bumped, books to fall, and general disruption to break out. With practice, students can make this transition quietly and efficiently. The teacher may decide to move the desks alone before or after school or to recruit a few student helpers.

Example:

Arrangement: Three desks pushed together to form a tablelike arrangement.

STEP 6: GIVE DIRECTIONS

In Step 6, the teacher states the specific assignment/task and provides each student with a handout. Repeat directions, and answer questions that students may have at this time.

Example:

Handouts: See the Activity Sheets in Figures 3.1, 3.2, and 3.3 in the Activity Sheet Appendix.

STEP 7: MONITOR GROUPS

Step 7 includes monitoring the students and checking both the group process and the students' product. This form of group guidance is similar to the usual monitoring of student group work done by effective teachers. The teacher provides assistance and clarification as needed. Also, the teacher reviews group skills and facilitates problem solving as needed.

Example:

Handouts: See Activity Sheet Appendix, Figures 3.1, 3.2, and 3.3.

After giving directions for the activities on Figures 3.1, 3.2, and 3.3, the teacher monitors groups and provides additional information as needed to help groups function more effectively.

STEP 8: PROVIDE CLOSURE

In Step 8, the teacher brings closure to the students' task or provides a transition to the next lesson activity. Various types of closure exist.

Ways to Provide Closure

1. The teacher asks for group summary reports from each group.
2. The teacher asks for individual reports from students chosen from groups.
3. One student from only one group shares with the whole class.
4. The teacher provides an overall summary at the end of the task.
5. The teacher leads a recitation session, asking questions and receiving answers.
6. The teacher collects and grades the group product.

STEP 9: EVALUATE THE PROCESS AND/OR PRODUCT

There are two general types of feedback or evaluation available to the teacher—individual and group. One involves individual student feedback to the teacher. This can include student self-evaluation, teacher testing, or individual oral reports. In most cases, students must individually demonstrate their mastery of the important skills or concepts of the learning task.

The teacher can also look at the group's product and/or make a general observation of the group's process. The group may receive a reward, when appropriate, for good performance. A group work grade or effort grade may be applied to the students' grade records if the grade is a *bonus* and does not serve as a penalty for groups that do not work as effectively. No group should be penalized for working together.

Examples:

1. Teacher gives verbal praise to individuals and/or groups.
2. Constitution is printed in class newsletter to parents.
3. Constitution is placed on the bulletin board.

EVALUATION ACTIVITY

Procedure: The groups complete the activity sheets dealing with student rights (see Activity Sheet Appendix, Figures 3.1, 3.2, and 3.3). They tally their group's votes on each of the questions. The designated recorders report to the class while the teacher records each group's vote on the chalkboard or overhead projector. Any other rights suggested by the groups should be added.

Self-Evaluation: Each student will evaluate his or her own work in the group by using Activity Sheet—Evaluation (see Activity Sheet Appendix, Figure 3.4). Each group member will briefly share his or her self-evaluation with the other members of the group.

Voting: The teacher will copy each group's ideas onto a large sheet of white paper or onto the chalkboard. All ideas should be phrased positively ("students in this class have a right to …" rather than "students in this class do not have a right to . . ."). Students will vote individually on the entire Classroom Constitution to decide if it should be adopted. If most agree, a copy of the Classroom Constitution should be displayed in the room, and all students should be given the opportunity to sign it.

Follow-Up: As time goes on, the teacher observes students and gives feedback on how well they are following the Classroom Constitution.

If necessary, small group meetings can be called in which students evaluate how well each right is being respected.

STEP 10: MAINTAIN CLASSROOM MANAGEMENT

Step 10 involves the teacher's classroom-management decisions. As William Glasser (1986) indicates, the more power you give students, the more power you have in the classroom. In the cooperative learning classroom, when the teacher allows students to control a part of their education, the teacher will have fewer discipline problems and actually have a more harmonious classroom setting. Although students will tend to become highly involved and motivated through working on their own product, the teacher needs to encourage specific criteria for *group* success that add up to a well-managed classroom. The following skills are described to the students and noted by the teacher.

Example:

1. Use a voice level that can be heard within the group but not outside the group.
2. Demonstrate good listening skills by hearing and recognizing what other students are saying.
3. Encourage group members to share and add ideas to the task.
4. Practice assigned roles and help others to carry out their assigned roles in an appropriate manner.

STEP 11: PLAN FOR ANALYSIS, REVIEW, AND MODIFICATION

Step 11 involves planning. After every lesson, the teacher analyzes and reviews the lesson with the goal of improving the lesson next time it is taught. A part of this planning process could involve student feedback. In most cases, the teacher makes notations in the plan book or unit/lesson folder of the changes that need to be made.

Example:

The teacher observes students and tells them how well they are following the Classroom Constitution. The teacher could lead periodic group discussions to allow students to evaluate which rights are being respected and which rights are not.

CONCLUSION

This step-by-step process contains the necessary components for implementing a cooperative learning lesson/unit of student interaction. Cooperative learning strategies are well researched and should form a part of any teacher's instruction. Group interaction found in cooperative learning is an important aspect of building a positive supportive classroom environment.

SELECTED REFERENCES

Featherstone, H. 1986. "Cooperative Learning." *Harvard Education Letter* September 4–6.

Foyle, H. C., and Lyman, L. 1993. *The Interactive Classroom.* (Videotape set: Part 1–Cooperative learning: Overview; Part 2–Cooperative learning: A step-by-step approach.) Washington, D.C.: National Education Association.

Fritz, J. 1987, *SHH! We're Writing the Constitution.* New York: G. P. Putnam's Sons.

Glasser, W. 1986. *Control Theory in the Classroom.* New York: Harper and Row, Publishers.

Gough, P. 1987. "The Key to Improving Schools: An Interview with William Glasser." *Phi Delta Kappan* (May) 656–62.

Lyman, L., and Foyle, H. C. 1988. "Cooperative Learning: Experiencing the Constitution in Action." Paper presented at the Rocky Mountain Regional Social Studies Conference, Salt Lake City, Utah, April 8–9. (ERIC Document Reproduction Service Number ED 293-791.)

_____ 1989. "Cooperative Learning Strategies and Children." (ERIC Digest Number EDO-PS-88-5.)

_____ 1990. "The Constitution in Action: A Cooperative Learning Approach." *Georgia Social Science Journal,* 21(1), 23–34.

Lyman, L., Wilson, A., Garhart, K., Heim, M., and Winn, W. 1987. *Clinical Instruction and Supervision for Accountability.* Dubuque, Iowa: Kendall/Hunt Publishing Company.

Slavin, R. 1987. "Cooperative Learning: Can Students Help Students Learn?" *Instructor,* March 74–78.

Chapter 4

SOCIAL SKILLS AND CONFLICT MANAGEMENT

Preventing conflicts is the work of politics; establishing peace is the work of education.

—*Maria Montessori*

One of the teacher's most important tasks in implementing cooperative learning in the elementary classroom is helping students to acquire, refine, and use social skills. Social skills are the tools students use to interact cooperatively. These skills can be taught and practiced within the medium of cooperative learning groups.

In the upper elementary grades, students can be taught to use social skills effectively within the classroom and to apply the skills to interactions outside of the classroom. Students can also become more active in solving the inevitable conflicts that arise when individuals work together.

SOCIAL SKILLS

Working in cooperative learning groups requires students to perform a number of social skills. By observing students during group-building activities, the teacher can begin to assess which skills will need to be taught or reinforced so that students in a particular classroom can work together effectively. Following are some of these important social skills.

Social Skills for Elementary Students

1. Students will share materials, resources, and space with group members and with other groups in the classroom.
2. Students will use appropriate voice levels when working in groups.
3. Students will listen attentively to other students when they are sharing ideas.

4. Students will participate appropriately in the group (not dominating the group, not letting others do all the work, practicing assigned roles).
5. Students will stay on task and make appropriate use of time.
6. Students will check to make sure other group members understand the ideas or skills the group is working on.
7. Students will accept differences of opinion and personality with other students in the group.
8. Students will disagree with other group members' ideas when necessary without putting them down.
9. Students will be able to explain and build on other group members' ideas.
10. Students will summarize the group's work and be able to share the group's ideas with other groups in the classroom.
11. Students will encourage other group members to share ideas and to participate in the group.
12. Students will help the group assess both the quality of its product(s) and the quality of its work together.

Other skills may be needed to help particular groups of students interact effectively.

Teaching Social Skills

Teachers can teach social skills by identifying the skill and the observable behaviors that will demonstrate that students are using it. For example, if a teacher has observed that students need to encourage each other as they work in groups, the teacher can ask students for words and phrases that are encouraging. Helping the students to think of specific examples is useful for students who have difficulty thinking of what to say. Having identified examples of the skill helps group members to recognize it when they use it in the group.

After the teacher makes a list of the students' words and phrases on the chalkboard or overhead projector, the teacher can present the cooperative learning task and ask students to encourage at least one other student while they are working on the task. The teacher should walk around and monitor the groups as they are working, giving feedback about how well students are working on both the task and social skill assigned.

At the end of the group's work, the teacher can ask students to share specific words or phrases that they used to encourage each other. This process may need to be repeated through several work sessions for a particular social skill to begin to become more automatic for students. It may also be necessary to review a particular skill from time to time. For this reason, it is helpful to record the ideas on an overhead transparency or on chart paper that can be saved for future reference.

The teacher may also wish to appoint a student in each group to observe and record his or her group's progress on a given social skill. The teacher can stop group work periodically and ask for the observer/recorder to give the group brief feedback. If the students are working on encouraging each other, for example, the observer/recorder can share examples of encouraging phrases they have used.

In some cases, the observer/recorder may use a tally sheet to keep track of the times each student practices the social skill. On the sample feedback sheet (see Activity Sheet Appendix, Figure 4.1), the observer/recorder would make a tally mark each time a group member said something encouraging to another group member and would write down examples of phrases that students used to encourage each other.

The feedback sheet can be adapted for other social skills as well. The teacher may also use a feedback sheet to record information about each group as he or she monitors the groups' work.

Social Skills Thematic Unit

A social skills thematic unit is a skill-based thematic unit that integrates seemingly diverse curricular areas around the goal of building social skills. Activities on a theme in several subject areas help students see relationships between their school subjects.

While the concept of thematic units is explored in more detail in Chapter 6, Integrating the Curriculum with Cooperative Learning, a skill-based thematic unit can be used to teach specific social skills to particular students. The following activities can be structured as a unit for the beginning of the year when students need help getting along with their new classmates.

SOCIAL SKILLS THEMATIC UNIT—GETTING ALONG WITH OTHERS

Skill:	Getting along with others (beginning of the school year)
Objectives:	Each student will interact with every other student in class in group-building activities that have a high probability of success. Students will practice procedures to be used in the classroom throughout the school year.
Procedure:	The teacher groups students with different students for each activity. Pairs or groups of three or four are used, depending on the cooperative skills of the students.

Sample Activities

Language Arts
1. Matching Game (Chapter 2)
2. Creature Feature (Chapter 2)
3. Communication Group-Builder (Chapter 2)
4. One for the Books (Chapter 4)

Math
1. Change for a Quarter (Chapter 4)
2. Two Dozen (Chapter 4)

Social Studies
1. Classroom Poll (Chapter 2)
2. Group Bulletin-Board (Chapter 4)

Science
1. Classifying Creatures (Chapter 4)
2. Common Senses (Chapter 4)

SOCIAL SKILLS THEMATIC UNIT—ONE FOR THE BOOKS

Objective:	Students will work together to identify words and phrases that contain the word book.

Procedure:	Students are grouped in pairs or in heterogeneous groups of three or four, depending on the skills of the class in cooperating. The teacher describes the task: groups will think of as many words or phrases that contain the word *book* as they can in the time provided. The teacher can ask the students to brainstorm some examples to get the groups started (see Activity Answers for examples).
	The teacher will also discuss and have students model appropriate voice levels for working together in groups. During the work time, the teacher will monitor the groups' voice levels and give feedback about how well each group is doing.
Follow-Up:	Because it is more important for groups to feel success in working together than to compete with each other, the teacher praises all groups for working well together, regardless of the number of answers obtained. Each group member should be asked to share something he or she liked about working with the other member(s) of the group before the group shares with the class. Groups can be asked to share with the class the total number of answers they thought of and one answer they feel is particularly creative. The teacher will also give the class feedback about how well they did in using appropriate voice levels during the group work.
Activity Answers:	book report, bookends, bookmobile, book cover, bookworm, booklet, bookstore, bookkeeper, bookmark, bookplate, bookshelf, reference book, matchbook, telephone book, baby book, scrapbook, hymn book, prayer book, fiction book, nonfiction book, mystery book, textbook, joke book, picture book, cookbook, book value, music book, comic book, make book on it, book a suspect, book a room, book a concert, booking office, bookbinding, bookbinder, hardback book, bookmaker, paperback book, blue book, book review, bestselling book, hit the books, book reviewer.

SOCIAL SKILLS—THEMATIC UNIT —CHANGE FOR
A QUARTER

Objective:	Students will identify possible coin combinations that add up to 25 cents.

Procedure:	Students are grouped in pairs or in heterogeneous groups of three or four, depending on the class's skill in cooperating. The teacher reviews the use of appropriate voice levels in the group, then asks students to model ways of encouraging group members to share ideas. The students are given the task of determining how many different combinations of coins they can come up with that equal 25 cents. While the students are working, the teacher monitors and gives each group feedback about how well members are encouraging each other to share ideas and how well they use appropriate voice levels to do so.

Follow-Up:	The teacher asks students to raise their hands to indicate that they contributed one or more of their group's answers, and the teacher praises the participation of the students. The teacher gives feedback to the class about voice levels and students' use of encouragement to each other in groups. The teacher has each group share one of its answers, then asks for additional answers from volunteer groups. It is helpful to list answers on an overhead or on the chalkboard so the groups will know which answers have already been given. Before ending the activity, each student should say something positive to his or her group about the work the group performed together.

Activity Answers:

1 (25), 5 (5), 25 (1)

1 (5), 20 (1)	2 (5), 15 (1)
3 (5), 10 (1)	4 (5), 5 (1)
1 (5), 2 (10)	3 (5), 1 (10)
15 (1), 1 (10)	5 (1), 2 (10)
10 (1), 1 (5), 1 (10)	5 (1), 2 (5), 1 (10)

(Numbers in parentheses indicate coin value. Other answers are possible if groups think of using foreign coins or early American coins.)

SOCIAL SKILLS THEMATIC UNIT—TWO DOZEN

Objective:	Students will determine appropriate mathematical operations necessary to make given number combinations total 24.

Procedure:	Students are grouped in pairs, or in heterogeneous groups of three or four, depending on the class's skill in cooperating. The teacher reviews the use of appropriate voice levels in the group,

then discusses and asks students to model ways of encouraging group members. The teacher discusses and has students share ideas about the ways students can share materials when resources are limited in groups. The teacher tells students that they will be working on an activity for which each group will have only one worksheet (see Activity Sheet Appendix, Figure 4.2). The group will need to take turns writing answers unless it appoints one person to do all the writing.

The teacher explains that each set of four numbers given on the worksheet can be combined with various math operations into a number sentence with the answer equalling 24 every time. The group must make each group of four numbers equal exactly two dozen (24) by inserting the appropriate operation signs for addition, subtraction, multiplication, or division. The groups may change the order of the numbers. They may use a given operation sign more than once in a given answer. But they may not leave out one of the numbers or use a number more times than it is given.

Example:

The teacher writes the numbers 3, 4, 5, and 5 on the chalkboard or overhead and helps the class find the solution.

One possible answer is $(5 \times 3) + 5 + 4 = 24$.

While the groups are working, the teacher should monitor the groups and give them feedback about their voice levels, their success in encouraging other group members to participate, and their ability to share the worksheet and the writing responsibilities.

Follow-Up:

As the teacher monitors the groups at work, he or she should check groups for correct answers and assign each group a problem to put on the chalkboard or overhead. The teacher then asks other groups to check answers for accuracy. Some groups may have found different and correct solutions to the same problem, and they should be encouraged to share those answers as well. The teacher asks for student feedback about how well the groups are working together, especially in (1) using *appropriate voice levels, (2) encouraging other group members to participate, and (3) sharing limited resources.*

45

Activity Answers:	Set 1. (1+2+3) x 4 = 24; (1x2) x (3x4) = 24; (4x2) x (3x1) = 24; (4x1) x (2x3) = 24
	Set 2. (4+2+2) x 3 = 24
	Set 3. (2x6) + (8+4) = 24; (6x8) ÷ (4-2) = 24
	Set 4. (2÷2) x (4x6) = 24
	Set 5. (3+5) + (7+9) = 24
	Set 6. (3x3x3) - 3 = 24
	Set 7. (4x4) + 4 + 4 = 24
	Set 8. 6 + 6 + 6 + 6 = 24
	Other answers may be possible.

SOCIAL SKILLS THEMATIC UNIT—GROUP BULLETIN BOARD

Objective: Students will learn geographical concepts.

Procedure: A map of your state, the United States, or the world is displayed on a bulletin board. Each student individually chooses two places that are of interest to him or her. Reasons for choosing a place can include finding the name interesting, having visited the place, having friends or relatives who live there, or having read about the place. After eliminating duplicates, the teacher has each student mark one place on the map with a map pin that gives the student's name and tells why the place is important to him or her. Example: "Eddie was born here"; "Wendy's grandmother lives here"; "Amy's favorite book took place here."

The teacher compiles a list of the places chosen by each student and uses the places to design activities to be completed in cooperative groups. If the students need practice in using an atlas, the following activities would be appropriate.

1. *Directions:* What direction would you travel from Wendy's grandmother's house to where Bob's family took its vacation? What direction would you travel from our school to the place where Amy's favorite book took place?

2. *Mileage:* Which of the special places are farthest north (south, east, west) from our school? How many miles would you travel from the place where Eddie was born to the place where Wendy's grandmother lives?

3. *Climates:* Which of the special places would have warm, dry climates? Which would have snow in the winter?

46

4. *Geographical Features:* Which of the special places are near an ocean (a lake, a river)? Which places are near mountains?

Students are grouped in pairs or in heterogeneous groups of three or four. The teacher models and discusses other classroom or cooperative group procedures that are needed, or reviews one of the previous skills that needs additional practice and instructs students to work on that skill while they complete the activity sheets. The teacher monitors groups and gives feedback to the groups as they are working.

Follow-Up: In the groups, each student should share at least one thing he or she thinks the group does well when it works together. The groups are instructed to decide what they did best in during the work period and share this with the class.

(Adapted from Lawrence Lyman and Harvey C. Foyle, *Journal of Geography*).

SOCIAL SKILLS THEMATIC UNIT—CLASSIFYING CREATURES

Objective: Students will classify given creatures as mammals, birds, fish, amphibians, reptiles, or insects.

Procedure: The teacher briefly helps the class review characteristics of mammals, birds, fish, amphibians, reptiles, and insects. The characteristics are listed on the chalkboard or overhead projector.

Students are grouped in pairs or in heterogeneous groups of three or four. The teacher models and discusses other classroom or cooperative group procedures that are needed, reviews a previous skill that has been worked on, or discusses and models a new skill for students to work on.

Students are instructed to use the corrected answers from the Creature Feature activity in Chapter 2. In their groups, the students classify each appropriately. The teacher monitors the groups as they are working and gives appropriate feedback.

Follow-Up: The teacher assigns groups to work with each other. The groups share answers. In the event of a disagreement, groups discuss and try to reach agreement. The teacher asks the groups to discuss and then share at least one positive thing that happened as they worked together.

Objective: Students will identify familiar things associated with the five senses.

Procedure: Students are grouped in pairs or in heterogeneous groups of three or four. The teacher models and discusses other classroom or cooperative group procedures that are needed, reviews a previous skill that has been worked on, or discusses and models a new skill for students to work on.

Each group is given a copy of Activity Sheet—The Common Senses (see Activity Sheet Appendix, Figure 4.3). The teacher should instruct the groups to either appoint one student as recorder or to take turns writing answers. The teacher tells the groups to think of at least one creative response for each item on the sheet—that is, a response other groups won't think of.

Follow-Up: Each group is assigned another group to work with. The groups compare answers to see how many original ideas each group thought of. After the groups are finished working, each group discusses and shares one positive thing about working together.

DEALING WITH STUDENT CONFLICT

Conflict is present in every setting where people work together. In the classroom, conflict can result in hurt feelings, problems in cooperative interaction, and even violence among students. Teachers can make the classroom safer and more pleasant and help students acquire human relations skills that will be important throughout their lives by teaching methods of dealing with conflict.

It is helpful for students to realize that conflict is a normal and predictable part of human interaction. In the following activity, students will recall famous conflicts that have taken place throughout history.

Objective: Students will identify famous conflicts.

Procedure:	Students are grouped in pairs or in heterogeneous groups of three or four. Each group is given Activity Sheet—Famous Conflicts (see Actvity Sheet Appendix, Figure 4.4). Students are instructed to work together to identify the person, character, or group that did not get along with the person or persons on the worksheet. Because some of the people will be unfamiliar to students, let them know that they are not expected to get all of the answers correct; suggest that they skip items they do not know.
Follow-Up:	The teacher could extend the assignment by giving groups several days to try to find answers through reference books, parents and other adult resources, or other strategies. At the end of the designated time, groups with the most correct answers can be rewarded.
	Groups can also be assigned to research a given conflict from the list and share a brief summary of it with the class.
Activity Answers:	(1) The Big Bad Wolf, (2) The Red Baron, (3) Bugs Bunny, (4) Abraham Lincoln, (5) The Montagues in Romeo and Juliet, (6) The Jets in West Side Story, (7) The Road Runner, (8) Peter Pan, (9) Alexander Hamilton, (10) Billie Jean King, (11) The McCoys, (12) Bluto, (13) Robin Hood, (14) Darth Vader, (15) Goliath, (16) Eliott Ness, (17) The United Federation of Planets (from the original Star Trek), (18) Cortez, (19) Moby Dick, (20) The Hare

It is also helpful for students to learn to recognize situations in which conflict commonly occurs. Figure 4.5 (see Activity Sheet Appendix) lists familiar types of conflict and examples. You may wish to review this sheet with students.

In the following activity, students learn about common types of conflict and think in groups of examples of each type.

SOCIAL SKILLS THEMATIC UNIT—CATEGORIZING CONFLICT

Objective:	Students will identify common situations that often produce conflict and think of an original example for each situation.

Procedure:	The teacher describes common types of conflict and gives some examples. Students are grouped in heterogeneous groups of three or four students. Each group is given a copy of Activity Sheet—Categorizing Conflict (see Activity Sheet Appendix, Figure 4.6). The group's task is to identify the type of conflict in each example. Students should be instructed that, even though they may disagree, they should support their answers and try to reach agreement as a group.
Follow-Up:	Groups can think of another example of each type of conflict.
Activity Answers:	(1) opinions or perceptions, (2) safety or right/wrong, (3) limited resources, (4) personalities/customs, (5) sharing people, (6) safety or right/wrong, (7) unfairness or unkindness, (8) safety or right/wrong, (9) personalities/customs, (10) unfairness or unkindness

The ability to understand the point of view of others is another essential skill in conflict management. In the following activity, students have the opportunity to take a nontraditional point of view and try to support it.

SOCIAL SKILLS THEMATIC UNIT—SEEING THE OTHER SIDE

Objective:	Given a nontraditional point of view, students will give reasons to defend it.
Procedure:	Students are grouped in heterogeneous groups of three or four. The teacher has the following tasks printed on index cards and each group draws a task. Each group reviews the story (have resources available if some stories are not as familiar). Each group comes up with three or more reasons for its assigned point of view. After the students have completed the task, the teacher has each group share its ideas with the class.
	Tasks: (1) Defend the wolf in *Little Red Riding Hood;* (2) Defend the trolls in *The Three Billy Goats Gruff;* (3) Defend the witch in *Snow White;* (4) Defend the stepsisters in *Cinderella;* (5) Defend the witch in *Hansel and Gretel;* (6) Defend the wolf in *The Three Little Pigs.*

As students disagree in classroom discussions, they can be asked to explain the point of view of a student with whom they disagree. The other student must agree that the point of view is fairly represented.

CLASSROOM MEETINGS AND STUDENTS AS MEDIATORS

As students learn to understand conflicts better, they can be taught specific strategies for resolving their own conflicts. Classroom meetings, where students work together to identify and solve classroom problems, are used by many elementary teachers to manage conflict and teach problem-solving skills. Students can also be taught to help each other solve disputes and conflicts by using peer mediation.

The agenda for a classroom meeting is developed cooperatively by students and the teacher. Individuals or groups who have an agenda item for a group meeting may submit it to the teacher in advance. The agenda items are discussed in the order submitted unless the class agrees that a certain problem should be discussed first.

In a classroom meeting, students sit in a circle. The teacher models procedures for speaking during the meeting, disagreeing constructively, and reaching agreement. The teacher should emphasize that the goal of the classroom meeting is to find "win/win" solutions; that is, solutions that benefit everyone. It may be helpful to develop a list of guidelines with the students for classroom meetings that can be reviewed periodically.

The classroom meeting shares both power and responsibility with students. The students have power to suggest problems and discuss them in a productive way. They also realize that the teacher is not solely responsible for resolving classroom problems. Participation in classroom meetings helps students to (1) learn important skills for solving problems, (2) develop feelings of ownership for their classroom, and (3) gain respect for their fellow students and teacher.

Students can also be taught skills of peer mediation that help solve disputes between individuals. For example, strategies for teaching peer mediation to students have been developed by Johnson and Johnson (1991).

CONCLUSION

Teachers cannot assume that their students have the necessary social skills for successful participation in cooperative groups, even if the students have previously worked in cooperative learning groups in other classrooms. The acquisition of social skills through cooperative learning is a process that must be actively facilitated by the teacher in order to be successful.

One of the advantages of cooperative learning is that students learn skills that are directly applicable to the inevitable individual and group conflicts that occur in the classroom. By teaching conflict management strategies and using classroom meetings, teachers can encourage classroom harmony and help students acquire important skills for future participation in a democratic society.

SELECTED REFERENCES

Johnson, D. W., and Johnson, R. T. 1987. *Creative Conflict*. Edina, Minn.: Interaction Book Company.

_____ 1991. *Teaching Children to be Peacemakers*. Edina, Minn.: Interaction Book Company.

Kriedler, W. J. 1984. *Creative Conflict Resolution: More Than 200 Activities for Keeping Peace in the Classroom K-6*. Glenview, Ill.: Good Year Books.

_____ 1990. *Elementary Perspectives I: Teaching Concepts of Peace and Conflict*. Cambridge, Mass.: Educators for Social Responsibility.

Lyman, L., and Foyle, H. 1991. "Teaching Geography Using Cooperative Learning," *Journal of Geography*, 90:5, 223-26.

Rhoades, J., and McCabe, M. 1992. *The Cooperative Classroom: Social and Academic Activities*. Bloomington, Ind.: National Educational Service.

Schniedwin, N., and Davidson, E. 1987. *Cooperative Learning, Cooperative Lives: A Sourcebook of Activities for Building a Peaceful World*. Somerville, Mass.: Circle Books.

Chapter 5

DRILL AND PRACTICE

When you are not practicing, remember: someone some-
where is practicing, and when you meet him, he will win.
—Ed MacAuley

In the elementary classroom, students need to work on tasks and practice skills that may seem routine and boring to them. Practice for practice's sake may not be a lofty educational goal. However, in the global society, other people are practicing until that which is practiced is overlearned and becomes routine. In this context, cooperative learning can be used to keep students working together on a task, practicing repetitive but important skills in different subject areas. Practice activities will also help teachers make productive use of unexpected blocks of classroom time by using "sponge activities."

USING PREPARED MATERIALS

A common task given to students in many elementary classrooms is to "answer the questions at the end of the chapter." Students with good reading skills can easily remember answers or can quickly look back at the chapter, and their task is often readily completed. Others who have more difficulty in reading and comprehending material may take much longer and be less successful in answering such questions. Even for the more skilled students, such exercises often do not result in long-term remembering or higher level understanding of the material being studied.

One cooperative strategy that the teacher can use with end-of-chapter exercises, workbook activities, and other prepared materials is to assign some of the work to be done together in heterogeneous groups. Students should be instructed that their group task is to make sure all students understand the answers the group writes for each question or problem, not simply to write answers or solve the problem.

Assigning roles to students as they work together on prepared materials can alleviate the problem of one student doing all of the work. One student can be assigned to write answers for the group, for example, while another can check the answers for accuracy. Another student can be the encourager, noticing other members' participation and praising thoughtful answers or helpful behaviors. One student can act as facilitator for the group, watching the time, making sure the group is on task, getting needed materials, and so on.

Individual accountability encourages student participation as the students work together on a given task. The teacher may wish to call on individual members of the group to give information during class discussions. The individual group members know that they must work together in understanding the material if their group is to be well represented in class discussions.

Individual mastery of content is facilitated by having students do a portion of the task by themselves or by giving a follow-up assignment based on earlier group work. Periodic tests and quizzes given by the teacher also provide feedback about how well individuals are mastering the material.

It is the position of the authors that only the individual work done by the student should be graded. Parents of talented students object when their child's grade is lowered because the group did not work well together, and the cooperative atmosphere of the classroom can be destroyed if students feel that cooperating together hurts their individual grade.

Group rewards other than grades are helpful as students work together on tasks in the classroom. In the case of prepared materials, the most obvious reward is that students have help in doing the work. The task is less cumbersome when others pitch in to get it done. Another built-in reward of cooperation is the fun of working together, talking about the subject rather than working silently and alone.

Slavin (1991) suggests that individual improvement scores on tests and quizzes can be used to recognize groups that work well together. This strategy rewards each member of the group for his or her effort and improvement rather than for academic ability. Using this strategy, it is possible for any student to help the team earn a good team score if he or she puts forth effort and makes improvement. Even students who are already doing well are encouraged to improve to help their teams. The specific strategies of Student Teams-Achievement Divisions (STAD) and Teams-Games-Tournaments (TGT) are explained in more detail in Slavin 1991.

USING STUDENT-GENERATED QUESTIONS

Students can generate their own questions and problems that can be solved cooperatively. After assigning a particular story or chapter or explaining a concept or strategy, the teacher places students in heterogeneous groups. Then the groups record their own questions or problems based on the content or concept studied. On a separate sheet, the group writes appropriate answers or responses to the questions members have just raised.

Then each group exchanges sheets with another group and tries to solve that group's questions or problems. The group generating the questions is responsible for providing feedback to the group answering them. The teacher monitors the groups and provides feedback about their work. He or she may edit student-generated questions or problems.

When students generate their own questions or problems, they are forced to think more critically about the structure and attributes of the content. Students also feel more powerful when they help to define problems related to content. They are learning important study skills that are applicable throughout their school careers.

Using Flash Cards

Flash cards are useful for learning basic math facts and can be used in other academic areas. Students can make flash cards on 3 x 5 inch cards or on scrap paper. The typical flash card has a fact on one side of the card and corresponding information on the other.

Flash cards need to be used appropriately. Following are some suggestions for pairs of students working with flash cards:

FIGURE 5.1
EXAMPLES OF VARIOUS SUBJECTS FOR FLASH CARDS

Math	3 x 7	21
English	beautiful (vocabulary word)	adjective (part of speech)
Science	frog alcohol	amphibian depressant
Social Studies	Kansas Plymouth	Topeka English colony
Foreign Language	perro	dog
Music	♪	eighth note

1. Let one student be the "teacher" with the flash cards for a short time, then switch roles.
2. The students should place any flash cards they miss in a "review pile" to be gone over again. It is important to recongize that many students will not review the facts that are missed unless taught to do so.
3. If a mistake occurs, the student who is acting as "teacher" should be taught to help the student identify the information to which the "wrong" answer applies. For example, if a student says "5 x 8 is 45," the student who is helping might say, "5 x 8 is 40, 5 x 9 is 45."
4. Individual accountability should be encouraged by using individual tests.

Card Kits

Kits of cards can be made to review geographic facts or famous people. To make a map kit, for example, the teacher selects the map of a state or country the class is studying. The map is cut into small pieces with each piece containing part of an individual county (state map) or state/province/region (national map). Each piece is glued to a 3 x 5 index card that is numbered and laminated. Each card should show at least three clues to the location of the place (e.g., names of cities, bodies of water, highways). Students work in cooperative groups to locate the county or state represented by as many different map pieces as possible.

Kits of cards can also be made for world leaders, scientists, inventors, or other celebrities the class is studying. The students can help by collecting pictures of celebrities from magazines. These pictures are glued on 3 x 5 cards, numbered, and laminated. The person's accomplishments can also be printed on the card. Each group is given a name list and matches as many cards as possible with the correct names.

COOPERATION WITH HOMEWORK

Some students have considerable trouble completing homework assignments accurately. What seemed easy to understand in the classroom may be confusing when the student attempts to work alone. If the teacher has difficulty getting homework assignments graded promptly, students will not get needed feedback in a timely manner.

Individual accountability can be maintained while allowing students to cooperate to complete their homework assignments. The teacher monitors the students' understanding and ability to work productively and gives an assignment such as solving 25 math problems. After explaining the assignment and doing sample problems with the class, the teacher assigns heterogeneous groups of two, three, or four students.

As the groups work on the problems, the teacher moves through the room, giving feedback and correction as appropriate. The teacher should give enough time so that all groups can complete at least five problems together. A built-in reward for groups that work well together is that they finish more of the assignment and have less to do at home.

Students do the remaining problems on their own. The next day, the teacher randomly selects five of the remaining problems and has the group members share their answers with one another and correct as needed. The advantage of this group discussion is that students get feedback about errors they have made without waiting for the teacher to correct, record, and return the papers. The teacher can then grade the remaining problems if he or she chooses or can randomly select one or two problems to spot check on each paper.

Groups that work particularly well together may get more of the work done together. This saves individual homework. Individual accountability is maintained by periodic quizzes or tests. Groups can be rewarded when members do well on these quizzes or tests.

Review Games

Cooperative games are enjoyable ways to summarize and review material for a test or to review a concept or skill after a period of time. Most simple game structures can be adapted to cooperative review. For example, suppose the teacher wants to review material that was taught about Christopher Columbus as part of a social studies unit.

A simple memory game will help review basic facts about Columbus. With class input, the teacher lists 10 facts about Columbus on the chalkboard or overhead and lists the information that goes with that fact. Facts and information are then copied on a 20-square grid as in Figure 5.2 (see Activity Sheet Appendix).

Students cut out the facts and information and mix the cards face down on a desk. Working in pairs, the students take turns turning over two cards at a time. If the information on the two cards matches, the student keeps the cards. The student with the most cards at the end of the game is the winner.

Cards can be replaced by blocks of wood. Review information is written on wooden blocks, and a game is played that allows students to practice or overlearn basic information.

ACTIVITY—BLOCK REVIEW GAME

Objective: The students practice and review geographic terms in a game format.

Materials: Small blocks of wood (commercial game type or teacher-made)

Procedure: The teacher prepares small blocks of wood all of one size, which can vary from between two to six inches in length, one to two inches in width, and one-fourth to one inch in depth. Using two sides of each block, the teacher writes a term on one side and the corresponding definition on the other side. Terms and other definitions may be on the same side of the block for the purpose of variety. As many as three different types of review content can be placed on each block. If the subject were geography, for example, the teacher could pair terms such as peninsula and its definition, states and capitals, or nations and capitals. The terms and definitions can be as complex as the teacher feels is appropriate for the students.

In cooperative groups of four students, teams of two are established by the teacher. A stack is made of the blocks. The object is to pull a block out of the stack without making the stack fall. The teacher tells the students which set of terms and definitions on the blocks is to be used. If a team member causes the stack to fall, that team loses. If the stack does not fall, the student reads one side of the pair without looking at the other side. If the student reads a definition, the appropriate term must be stated by the partner for an award of one point. If the student reads a term and its definition is correctly stated by the partner, two points are awarded. Students keep their own scores. At the end of the game, one pair of students wins, and the highest score in the class is recognized.

Follow-Up Activity: The teacher gives a quiz or test on the terms for the purpose of individual accountability.

(Activity courtesy of Ed Abbuehl, sixth grade teacher, Eisenhower Middle School, Topeka Public Schools, Topeka, Kansas.)

SPONGE ACTIVITIES

Sponge activities are ideal topics for cooperative groups. In the following examples, students are grouped in pairs or heterogeneous groups of three or four. The teacher tells the group that its task is to write the names of cities, states, bodies of water, or nations in the box that begins with the letter at the top of the column (see Activity Sheet Appendix, Figure 5.3). For cities, for example, the students could write Frankfort for F, Indianapolis for I, New York City for N, and Denver for D. Groups try to get at least one response for each box. In this activity (Foyle and Lyman 1991), *water* includes rivers, lakes, oceans, seas, and straits.

CONCLUSION

Students may be unmotivated to work with prepared materials. They may be bored by the routine and repetition involved in learning essential facts. Teachers can use cooperative learning to help students work together on prepared materials, generating their own questions and problems and working more successfully on homework assignments. Flash cards, card kits, and cooperative review games can be used to keep students interested as they review content and practice essential study skills. Finally, sponge activities make a good classroom management tool, creating fun for students while they work together.

SELECTED REFERENCES

Foyle, H. C. 1989. *Homework: A Practical Teacher's Guide.* Portland, Maine: J. Weston Walch.

Foyle, H. C., and Lyman, L. 1991. "A Sponge Activity to Spark Student Interest." *Geographic Insights* 1(2), 9.

Hunter, M. C. 1973. "Make Each Five Minutes Count." *Instructor* 83(4), 97–98.

Slavin, R.E. 1991. *Using Student Team Learning,* 3rd edition. Baltimore, Md.: The Johns Hopkins Team Learning Project, Center for Research on Elementary and Middle Schools, Johns Hopkins University.

Chapter 6

INTEGRATING THE CURRICULUM WITH COOPERATIVE LEARNING

An idea is a feat of association.

—*Robert Frost*

Many educators are focusing on the need to make curriculum more meaningful to students so that they will learn more effectively and retain what they learn. Even when teachers use effective teaching strategies like cooperative learning, students can have difficulty relating math, reading, social studies, science, and other curriculum areas to each other.

TEACHING DESIRED OUTCOMES WITH THEMATIC UNITS

As school districts become more specific in determining instructional outcomes for grade levels and subject areas, teachers may feel they have fewer opportunities for creativity and flexibility. In fact, there are many strategies, materials, and topics that will produce the desired outcomes. If students must learn to identify nouns, the teacher can show them how to identify nouns in a reading or language arts textbook. But nouns can also be identified in science books, math books, social studies books, literature books, and real-life situations. As students see the applications beyond a specific subject area or school period, learning becomes more interesting and meaningful.

One strategy for integrating the elementary school curriculum is to teach intended outcomes in *thematic units*. A thematic unit integrates seemingly diverse subject areas by focusing on a topic, idea, or skill that is common to all. Teachers of one grade level can work together to create thematic units that are enjoyable for students and effective in reaching the desired learning outcomes for that grade level or subject.

Thematic units provide many opportunities for student interaction in cooperative groups. As student interest in learning increases, the opportunity to share ideas with other students is increasingly important. Students can also assume responsibility, under the direction of the teacher, for presenting material to their fellow students and for helping each other practice needed skills. Because many thematic units are teacher-designed, student feedback is important in helping to improve the unit and design other units.

TYPES OF THEMATIC UNITS

There are three types of thematic units: skill-based, experience-based, and topic-based.

A *skill-based* thematic unit uses different activities from as many subject areas as possible to practice a skill needed by the students. Such skills may include getting along with others, listening, making choices, or solving problems. In a skill-based thematic unit, selected activities are designed to help the students gain experience and confidence as they succeed with a particular skill. An example of a skill-based thematic unit is the social skills thematic unit found in Chapter 4.

An *experience-based* thematic unit focuses on a single event, such as a story, a field trip, a classroom event, a demonstration, or an experiment. Using an experience that the students in the classroom have shared as a base, activities are chosen to achieve particular objectives. Suggestions for creating experience-based thematic literature units are found in Chapter 10.

Topic-based thematic units are based on a high interest topic that focuses learning activities in varied subject areas. Teachers may choose the subject matter for a topic-based thematic unit based on their special experiences, skills, or interests. Two topic-based units are included in this chapter. They are: Advertising in Literature and *Mrs. Frisby and the Rats of NIMH* (ideas adapted from Margaret Davidson and Gwen Eidman).

To create a topic-based thematic unit, the teacher identifies learning outcomes to be achieved in each of the subject areas. The teacher then designs activities that will achieve those outcomes. In the following activities from a topic-based thematic unit, advertising was the topic that helped students reach objectives in a variety of subject areas. As students became aware of advertising techniques, they became better consumers. The familiarity of commercials kept elementary students interested in the topic.

TOPIC-BASED THEMATIC UNIT—ADVERTISING IN
LITERATURE

Advertising Strategies

Content Area:	Language arts
Objective:	Students will identify techniques used by advertisers to sell their products.
Procedure:	Students are given a copy of Activity Sheet—Advertising Strategies (see Activity Sheet Appendix, Figure 6.1). In cooperative groups, students think of examples of each type of commercial or advertisement.

Advertising Examples

Procedure:	After students have discussed the various advertising strategies, cooperative groups work together to find examples of the strategies in magazine and newspaper advertisements.
	The groups then pool their findings and list as many slogans as they can. The group must supply both the slogan and the product that the slogan represents. The teacher may wish to allow students to think about slogans for a day or two before asking the groups to share their slogans. Groups can be rewarded for thinking of the most slogans and for thinking of slogans other groups did not find.
Follow-Up:	Groups can think of an original product they would like to advertise and develop a commercial for it. The commercial should use at least two of the advertising strategies in Figure

6.1. After the commercial is performed, other groups can try to identify the strategies used in the commercial.

Advertising in Literature

Content Area:	Language arts
Objective:	Students will analyze fiction and nonfiction examples of advertising in literature.
Procedure:	Students are assigned cooperative groups. Each group is assigned a source that contains a fictional or true story about advertising. A list of stories about advertising is given below. Each group analyzes its selection by using the criteria in Activity Sheet—Advertising Analysis (see Activity Sheet Appendix, Figure 6.2).
Follow-Up:	The group members can share the completed analysis of their story with other groups.

Stories About Advertising

Baker, N. B. 1954. *Nickels and Dimes: The Story of F. W. Woolworth.* Scholastic. "Any Article, Five Cents," 60–68. "Woolworth's Five and Ten," 69–78.

Bond, M. 1974. *Paddington on Top.* Dell. "Keeping Fit," 74–88.

Cleary, B. 1957. *Henry and the Paper Route.* Morrow. "Henry's Advertisements," 75–102.

Hicks, C. B. 1976. *Alvin's Swap Shop.* Scholastic. "The Swap Shop," 36–45.

Klevin, J. R. 1982. *The Turtle Street Trading Company.* Dell. "Problems," 52–55. ". . . And More Problems," 56–62.

Krantz, H. 1961. *100 Pounds of Popcorn.* Scholastic. "Popcorn, Popcorn Everywhere," 24–33. "Movie Business," 40–47.

Robertson, K. 1970. *Henry Reed's Big Show.* Grosset and Dunlap. "Saturday Evening, June 28th," 90–100. "Monday, June 30th," 107–17.

Which Is the Best Value?

Content Area:	Math
Objective:	For several products, students will calculate the cost of two different brands to determine which is the greater value.
Procedure:	Students are grouped in cooperative groups. Each group is given Activity Sheet—Determining Best Value (see Activity Sheet Appendix, Figure 6.3) listing Brand A and Brand B products. By calculating the cost per ounce of each product, the group decides which product is the best value.
Follow-Up:	Students can compare their answers with other groups to see if they agree. Groups can then be given newspaper grocery advertisements from different stores to use to calculate which products are better values. For additional practice, complete the exercise in Activity Sheet—Best Value Soft Drink (see Activity Sheet Appendix, Figure 6.4).

Bonus Prizes

Content Area:	Social studies (economics)
Objective:	Students will analyze reasons why advertisers include bonus offers with products and then determine whether such bonuses are good values.
Procedure:	Students are assigned cooperative groups. Each group is given a copy of Activity Sheet—Bonus! Free! Prizes! (see Activity Sheet Appendix, Figure 6.5) for group discussion.
Follow-Up:	Group members bring in samples of inexpensive bonus items they received for buying a product or a meal. Groups estimate the cost of the bonus items and compare the price they paid to the price they would have paid without the "prize."

Public Opinion Polls

Content Area:	Social Studies and math
Objective:	Students will participate in a classroom poll and make a graph of part of the results of the poll.

Procedure:	Students complete the Classroom Poll activity in Chapter 2. After the data is collected, each group is assigned one question from the poll. The group members work together to make a graph of the data that was collected. Each graph is shared with the whole class.
Follow-Up:	Groups can poll members of other classes by using the questions on Activity Sheet—Bonus! Free! Prizes! (see Activity Sheet Appendix, Figure 6.5). Results can be shared with other groups.

Testing Products

Content Area:	Science
Objective:	Students will formulate a hypothesis about a product of their choice and design and conduct an experiment to test the hypothesis.
Procedure:	Students are assigned cooperative groups. Each group chooses a product it would like to test. For example, a group might choose to test two or more brands of paper towels to see which can absorb the most liquid. Each group must have its hypothesis and experiment approved by the teacher before conducting it.
Follow-Up:	Each group prepares a chart to share with the class, showing the results of its experiment.

Resources on Product Testing

Adams, A. H., Flowers, A., and Woods, E. E. 1978. *Reading for Survival in Today's Society,* volumes 1 and 2. Glenview, Ill.: Scott Foresman.

Weiss, A. E. 1979. *The School on Madison Avenue: Advertising and What It Teaches.* New York: Dutton.

TOPIC-BASED THEMATIC UNIT—MRS. FRISBY AND
THE RATS OF NIMH

Author's Purpose

Content Area:	Language arts, point of view, author's purpose

Objective:	After reading *Mrs. Frisby and the Rats of NIMH,* students will identify the person from whose point of view the story is told and the author's purpose for this story.
Procedure:	In cooperative groups, students will discuss the following two questions: (1) From whose point of view is this story told? (2) What is the author's purpose for writing this story? Students will discuss these questions until each group has two answers arrived at by consensus.

Social Studies

Content Area:	Social studies, point of view
Objective:	After reading *Mrs. Frisby and the Rats of NIMH* and two articles distributed by the teacher, students in cooperative groups will outline the concerns of scientists who develop drugs for human disease and animal-rights activists. Each group will write two editorials, one on each side of the issue.
Procedure:	After reading the story, the teacher provides the students with two short articles or teacher-written summaries of the scientist's viewpoint and the animal-rights activists' viewpoints on animal testing of drugs or cosmetics. In cooperative groups, students will write two newspaper editorials, one arguing in favor of animal testing of drugs and one arguing against animal testing of drugs.

Art

Content Area:	Art, point of view
Objective:	Students will become familiar with the painting style of Salvador Dali.
Procedure:	The teacher shows reproductions of one or two paintings of Salvador Dali to the class and provides some background information about the artist. As a class, students discuss the ways Dali represents various objects in his paintings. They then move into small cooperative groups of three or four students. The teacher gives each group of students a reproduction of a Dali painting. Students draw the objects in the painting from their own point of view to make a group painting.

Communication

Content Area: Communication, point of view

Objective: Students will describe what they see in a "double image" drawing to other members of their group.

Procedure: Students are each given a copy of a "double image" picture such as the well-known "chalice and two faces" or the "young woman/old hag." Students will look at only their picture. In turn, students will describe what they see and then turn the picture so that other students attempt to see what was described. After all pictures have been described, the teacher asks students to look for a second object in each picture. *Round Trip* and *Reflections* by Ann Jonas may also work well in this activity.

Critical Thinking

Content Area: Critical thinking, author's (producer's) purpose

Objective: After the reading the book, *Mrs. Frisby and the Rats of NIMH* and while watching the video version of *The Secrets of NIMH*, students will record differences between the two approaches, discuss them in cooperative groups, and determine the movie producers' purpose for the changes made between the book and the video.

Procedure: Students will read the book and watch the video. While watching the video, students will record every difference that they detect between the plot and characters in the book and the video. In cooperative groups, students will discuss the differences that they found and possible purposes (motives) for those changes. In a whole class discussion, each group will share the possible purposes (motives) for the changes.

Scientific Method

Content Area: Science, controlling variables

Objective: Students will conduct a science experiment controlling all the variables except the one variable being tested.

Procedure:	Students are given a copy of the Activity Sheet—Control a Variable (Activity Sheet Appendix, Figure 6.6). In cooperative groups, students will build whirlybirds (paper helicopters) out of four different materials: tissue paper, typing paper, oak-tag board, and cereal-box cardboard. The students will hypothesize about which whirlybird will fly the longest, the manner in which each will fly, and how long each will stay in the air. To test the hypothesis, the groups will then fly the whirlybirds three times, record their findings (data collection) on the activity sheet, and calculate the average for each whirlybird. The groups will then discuss their findings using the collected data (verification of hypotheses). Each group will share its work with the whole class. (See Scholastic, "Toy Testers" reference for additional ideas.)

Mathematics

Content Area:	Mathematics, graphing activity
Objective:	Students will construct a bar or a line graph that illustrates the data gathered in the whirlybird experiment.
Procedure:	The teacher provides the groups of students with graph paper. After explaining the importance of displaying scientific findings through the use of graphs, the teacher directs the students to make graphs of their data findings. Each group decides whether to use a bar graph or a line graph. The groups then graph their data and use the graphs in their presentation to the whole class.
Follow-Up:	A number of follow-up activities are possible in this unit. Students might read the sequel to *Mrs. Frisby and the Rats of NIMH* and compare the author's purpose in the two books. Students might collaborate on a sequel to the book that describes what happens to the rats living on their own. Students might design other activities to control variables.

Groups might produce a play or reader's theatre of an episode from the book. Students might write a "5 W and an H" (who, what, where, when, why, and how) poem about their favorite character in the books. Follow-up activities vary based upon the interests of students. The students are a source of many ideas for follow-up activities. In one sixth-grade class, students were so concerned about changes that the producers had made in the movie version of the book that they wrote the production company about their concerns.

CONCLUSION

Thematic units offer the teacher an opportunity to organize the curriculum in a way that is more meaningful to students. Students can become actively involved in thematic units through cooperative interaction in groups. When the curriculum is more meaningful to students, and the ways in which the curriculum is taught meet the needs and interests of students, students will learn more efficiently and remember what has been learned longer.

SELECTED REFERENCES

Brandt, R. S., (ed). 1991. Integrating the Curriculum (theme issue). *Educational Leadership* 49(2).

Jacobs, H. H., (ed). 1989. *Interdisciplinary Curriculum: Design and Implementation.* Alexandria, Va.: Association for Supervision and Curriculum Development.

Jonas, A. 1983. *Round Trip.* N.Y.: Scholastic.

_____ 1987. *Reflections.* N.Y.: Greenwillow.

Ontario Science Centre, (ed). *Scienceworks: 65 Experiments that Introduce the Fun and Wonders of Science.* Reading, Mass.: Addison-Wesley.

Scholastic, (ed.). 1989. "Toy Testers." *Super Science* (November/December). Jefferson City, Mo.: Scholastic.

The Secret of NIMH. MGM/UA home video production.

Thompson, G. 1991. *Teaching Through Themes.* Jefferson City, Mo.: Scholastic Professional Books.

Vars, G. F. 1987. *Interdisciplinary Teaching in the Middle Grades: Why and How.* Columbus, Ohio: National Middle School Association.

Chapter 7

APPRECIATING INDIVIDUAL AND CULTURAL DIFFERENCES

To me, the question of doing away with all race and religious bigotry in this country is the most important of all.

—Theodore Roosevelt

Appreciating individual and cultural differences has become one of the major goals of American society. A variety of educational terms describe this goal: multicultural education, ethnic studies, and cultural diversity. A resurgence of interest in multicultural education has been influenced by a number of factors, a major one being demographic changes among the school-aged population. The increase in the number of children considered members of ethnic or racial minority groups has dramatically increased. In 1976, for example, 24 percent of the total school enrollment in U.S. schools was nonwhite. That percentage increased to 29 percent by 1984 and is expected to be 33 percent by the year 2000. It is projected that by 2020, 46 percent of the school population will be nonwhite. In Colorado, Texas, New Mexico, California, and Arizona, the proportion of students classified as minorities already comprises more than 50 percent of the school populations. Unfortunately, recent race riots in several of our larger urban areas are another reason for renewed interest in multicultural education. The rise of teen gangs and violence among ethnic groups escalates our perception of interethnic conflict.

One basic approach to multicultural education is to emphasize improving communication and understanding among ethnic and cultural groups. Proponents of this model point out that the U.S. is a culturally diverse nation in which the participation of all Americans should be appreciated. This approach assumes that all social and ethnic groups are of equal importance. It stresses that appreciation of differences and similarities among all peoples is an important part of multicultural education.

Using cooperative learning, elementary teachers can help their students appreciate each other when differing factors such as gender, ethnicity, race, religion, culture, and physical attributes are present in the classroom. Research on cooperative learning has consistently indicated that increased liking and respect among students of diverse backgrounds is a positive outcome of this methodology (Slavin 1990). Considerable evidence suggests that cooperative learning strategies will improve intergroup relations in the classroom. For example, research reveals that when students of diverse backgrounds work together to achieve a common goal, they begin to understand one another better and respect one another more. Johnson and Johnson (1985) have stated:

> Cooperative learning experiences promote greater acceptance of differences and interpersonal attraction among students from different ethnic backgrounds and among handicapped and nonhandicapped students. Putting students in cooperative contact who might not ordinarily seek such interaction and having them work cooperatively moves students beyond initial prejudices toward other students to multidimensional views of one another. Furthermore, such experiences allow them to deal with each other as fellow students rather than as stereotypes.

It would appear from the research that multicultural education and cooperative learning strategies improve both student achievement and interpersonal relations among the various cultural and ethnic groups.

GROUP-BUILDING STRATEGY

An activity involving the cultural heritage of various nations and their impact on American life is the group builder, National Names. Although it oversimplifies cultural contributions to our language, elementary children find it interesting and motivating.

Objective: Students will identify influences of nationalities and cultures on American language. Students will be motivated to do further research on the impact of other nationalities and cultures on American life.

Material: Use Activity Sheet—National Names (see Actvity Sheet Appendix, Figure 7.1).

Procedure: The teacher divides the class into heterogeneous groups of three or four students. The groups discuss answers for the worksheet. The students may use any resources available to help find the missing word related to a particular nationality or culture.

Individual Accountability: Because this is a motivational activity, students should not be quizzed over this material.

Follow-Up: Groups of students can research various nationalities and cultures for their contributions to American life. Suggestions could come from the Activity Sheet—National Names, or from the students' own backgrounds and ideas. The teacher should observe the interest level of the students in order to determine if other motivational techniques should be used before beginning a research study.

GROUP-INVESTIGATION STRATEGIES

Another successful cooperative learning strategy is *group investigation* (Sharan and Sharan 1992), which has been specifically designed to foster appreciation of individual and cultural differences among children. Many upper elementary teachers have tried assigning reports on a state or country of the student's choosing. In some cases, the reports are not done well and students do not interact appropriately. Group investigation is a research approach that deals directly with these concerns. Students follow a series of six steps directed by the teacher over a given period of time. The process includes:

1.   *Topic Identification.* The teacher and/or the students identify research topics. The teacher may indicate the general area of study such as a period in history. The students may brainstorm indi-

vidually or in groups to come up with the names of historical persons to study (example: Cesar Chavez).

2. *Small Group Planning.* The teacher divides the class into small groups. These small groups are responsible for developing the subtopics that relate to the person who is being investigated. The students may examine their textbook or other resources and come up with a variety of subtopics, such as California, Texas, farm workers, unions, lettuce, and grapes.

3. *The Investigation.* The students begin to gather information. They may divide their material into subtopics or work on all the topics together. They may share information with other groups, discuss the information, and generally become knowledgeable about the subject. For example, one student in the Cesar Chavez group might look for information about what Chavez had to do with farming.

4. *The Group Report.* The students make a report to the class on the information they have found. They may use any active participation approach (example: skits about farm workers picking lettuce). During this preparation time, students discuss the best way to present the researched information. Each group and each individual in the group assists in reporting to the class. The class watches, listens, takes notes, asks questions, and absorbs the other groups' reports. The students might ask such specific questions as, "How much money did the farm workers get paid for picking lettuce?"

6. *Evaluation.* As in most cooperative learning strategies, the students may appraise their own individual work, the group's work, and the class's work. Teachers often use written essay evaluations, checklists, and observation sheets. Innovative evaluation can take place, such as drawing a picture of the class in action, or drawing a picture that captures the key ideas of the reports. Normal quizzes and tests are often—but not always—given to the students.

An example of a group-investigation approach is given in the activity, Some Important People. Students need to become aware that important people come from all genders, racial groups, ethnic and cultural groups, religious groups, and age groups.

ACTIVITY—SOME IMPORTANT PEOPLE

Objective: Students will note that important people come from all genders, racial groups, ethnic and cultural groups, religious groups, and age groups. They will do research and report on the contributions of a sampling of these important people.

Material: Activity Sheet—Some Important People (see Activity Sheet Appendix, Figure 7.2) lists some important historical people. By changing the list, the activity can be repeated from time to time during the school year.

Procedure: Following the group-investigation procedure, the teacher hands out Activity Sheet—Some Important People (Figure 7.2). Students will do research and report on these people. The teacher comments that some of these names may be difficult to find and little information may be available in such standard resources as encyclopedias and textbooks. Students may consult with parents or other human resources. The teacher may also take students to the library for further research.

Individual Accountability: The teacher may quiz the students on the reports.

Follow-Up: From time to time, provide a different list of important people's names for students to research.

Another approach to sharing information about cultures and people is to show slides or exhibit artifacts that represent a particular ethnic group. Most communities have adults who have travelled to other nations or who are members of various ethnic and racial groups. These people can be invited to make presentations to the class. The teacher designs a cooperative learning activity that would involve the students before, during, or after the presentation. For example, a traveler returning from a trip to Japan may bring photographs, postcards, and various items to share with the class. The teacher follows the procedure in the next activity. It is based on a cooperative learning strategy called *learning together* (Johnson and Johnson 1991).

ACTIVITY—JAPANESE ARTIFACTS

Objective: Students will make a connection between presented information about Japan and artifacts from that culture.

Materials: Any Japanese artifacts, such as pictures, books, boxes, bags, cans, toys, goods, clothes

Procedure: The teacher arranges the students into heterogeneous groups of three or four students. Each group is given a Japanese artifact to examine. The students discuss how the artifact relates to the presentation on Japan. The students discuss similarities and differences between the Japanese artifact and its American counterpart, not of Japanese origin, such as a Japanese hand painted fan versus a hand fan with advertisements found in church pews in some parts of the United States. The students may write down their observations and report to the class when called upon by the teacher.

Individual Accountability: Students might be individually called upon by the teacher to explain a similarity or difference between the Japanese artifact and a comparable U.S. artifact. This individual verbal feedback would be sufficient to assess the involvement of specific students in the group's discussion.

Follow-Up: Use this format to relate information on any culture to artifacts of that cultural, ethnic, or racial group.

CONCLUSION

Cooperative learning is an ideal classroom methodology for encouraging positive interactions among children. Groups of students who are from varying backgrounds, cultures, races, and ethnic groups can learn to work together when focusing on a common goal and task.

SELECTED REFERENCES

Banks, J. A. 1981. *Multi-ethnic Education: Theory and Practice.* Boston, Mass.: Allyn and Bacon.

_____ 1979. *Teaching Strategies for Ethnic Studies,* 2nd edition. Boston, Mass.: Allyn and Bacon.

Conrad, B. D. 1985. "Multicultural Education Through Student Team Learning." *Journal of Staff Development* (October).

_____ 1988. "Cooperative Learning and Prejudice Reduction." *Social Education* (April/May).

Diaz, Carlos, ed. 1992. *Multicultural Education for the 21st Century.* Washington, D.C.: National Education Association.

Johnson, D. W., and Johnson, R. 1991. *Learning Together and Alone: Cooperative, Competitive, and Individualistic Learning,* 3rd edition. Englewood Cliffs, N.J.: Prentice-Hall.

_____ 1985. "Student-Student Interaction: Ignored but Powerful." *Journal of Teacher Education* 36(4): 23.

Ladestro, D. 1991. "Teaching Tolerance." *Teacher Magazine* 2(5): 26–27.

Richard-Amato, P., and Snow, M. A., eds. 1992. *The Multicultural Classroom.* N.Y.: Longman.

Sharan, Y., and Sharan, S. 1992. *Expanding Cooperative Learning Through Group Investigation.* New York: Teachers College Press.

Slavin, R. E. 1990. *Cooperative Learning: Theory, Research, and Practice.* Englewood Cliffs, N.J.: Prentice-Hall.

Chapter 8

PROBLEM SOLVING AND CRITICAL THINKING

Knowledge is the most powerful problem-solving tool there is. If I want to solve problems in mathematics, I've got to have mathematical concepts. But there's a difference between teaching knowledge as a tool that facilitates problem solving and teaching it simply as a thing to be memorized.

—John Bransford

When solving a problem, we may use critical-thinking skills. Critical thinking can be a form of convergent thinking, seeking a single response or solution. Critical thinking pursues the one correct or most acceptable solution. While cooperative learning makes the most of problem-solving strategies, it also includes much more. This chapter will demonstrate the interaction of critical thinking (problem solving) with cooperative learning.

THINK-PAIR-SHARE

A simple cooperative learning strategy called Think-Pair-Share (Lyman 1992) works well with students who are problem solving. Think-Pair-Share is based on the concept that every student must participate and that, given enough time, students will provide accurate answers. Various examples of this technique are found in Frank Lyman's *Think-Pair-Share* videotape (Lyman 1993). Think-Pair-Share derives its name from the process itself.

- *Think.* After a teacher's question, some students immediately blurt out incorrect answers, and brighter students may burst out with the correct answer. Because they are primarily interested in sharing, students have not had enough time to think through their response. In the think mode, students quietly read, reflect upon an answer, or work out a problem alone.

- *Pair.* When the teacher signals for the pair mode, students get together with a partner to combine their thinking or problem solving. Students are highly involved in the learning process as they take turns explaining their knowledge to their partner.

- *Share.* When each student has had time to consider a partner's thinking about the problem, it is time to share with the whole class. At this point, student responses are usually more thoughtful because they were discussed in advance with another student. Also, students are interested in how closely their responses match those of other pairs. If a pair of students happens to be incorrect, other pairs shed light on the question or problem.

Problem-solving and critical-thinking skills can be enhanced by using Think-Pair-Share as a cooperative learning strategy. The use of Think-Pair-Share is suggested in the following mathematics, social studies, language arts, and science activities.

MATHEMATICS

Prior to a mathematics lesson, the teacher assigns a group builder such as Activity Sheet—Numbers (see Activity Sheet Appendix, Figure 8.1). This simple activity not only provides an anticipatory set for the coming lesson but it also gives children practice with Think-Pair-Share strategy.

Individually in the think mode, the students put the numbers on Activity Sheet—Numbers in order. Then in the pair mode, partners compare their answers. Students will learn the answers for items they did not know, for example, the number of kids in *The Brady Bunch*. After the pairs have compared answers, the teacher moves the class into the share mode by asking for responses from selected pairs of students.

Now that the students have practiced Think-Pair-Share, they are ready for a more complicated mathematics lesson. Think-Pair-Share can use textbook story-problems or enrichment problems selected by the teacher. The following example turns the song, "The 12 Days of Christmas," into a mathematics problem.

ACTIVITY—THE 12 DAYS OF CHRISTMAS

Objective: The students will solve a story problem related to the seasonal song, "The 12 Days of Christmas" and determine the total number of gifts given.

Materials: A recorded version of the song, "The 12 Days of Christmas" or the written words for the song. Calculators may be used if the teacher desires.

Procedure: The teacher indicates to the students that they will be working with partners in a Think-Pair-Share activity. The teacher may pre-assign partners in order to place students strong in mathematics with students who need help. After playing the song, "The 12 Days of Christmas," or handing out the lyrics, students work individually on the problem (think mode).

What is the total number of gifts given during the 12 days? When students have completed their private calculations, they join their partners (pair mode) and determine who has the correct answer and how it was arrived at. Some teachers may allow students to assist each other during the think mode if one of the students is stuck on the problem or needs a hint. When the pairs of students have finished comparing answers and strategies, the teacher calls pairs of students to the board to show their answers for each of the 12 days. Finally, the pairs write the total number of gifts for all 12 days (share mode).

Even though this process takes time, it gives the students consistent and immediate feedback from each other and the teacher. In addition, the students are not as embarrassed about presenting incorrect information and being laughed at by other students. Finally, the students who might have been left out of the process feel a sense of accomplishment from working in front of the class.

Individual Accountability: The teacher supervises students during the think mode, helping them as they individually work on the problem. A similar problem may be given as a test or quiz after a story-problem unit or series of lessons, in order to evaluate the retention of individual students.

| *Follow-Up:* | Once students become comfortable with the Think-Pair-Share *process*, and succeed at coming up with the correct answers and procedures (the *product*), the teacher may continue to use the process with story problems found in textbooks, teacher's manuals, or enrichment materials. |

SOCIAL STUDIES

To prepare students for a Think-Pair-Share social studies lesson and practice the Think-Pair-Share strategy, the group builder Great may be used. Teachers follow the Think-Pair-Share steps outlined above. Each student receives a copy of the Activity Sheet—Great (see Activity Sheet Appendix, Figure 8.2), which asks them to identify a list of 10 "greats." Next, pair the students for more complete answers. The teacher monitors the students, and when they have completed as much of the sheet as they can, the teacher asks pairs to share with the whole class.

After practicing Think-Pair-Share, the students may move on to more complex problem-solving lessons. The teacher will find such lessons in the social studies textbook or other social studies materials. Team Category Challenge is a sample of a more complex lesson.

ACTIVITY—TEAM CATEGORY CHALLENGE

Objective:	The students will come up with four answers that fit the category that is related to a letter of the alphabet.
Materials:	Activity Sheet—Team Category Challenge, (Figure 8.3), and Team Category Challenge Answers (Figure 8.4). See Activity Sheet Appendix.
Procedure:	Individual students write down as many terms that fit the category in the boxes labeled Answer 1, Answer 2, Answer 3, and Answer 4 (think mode). After the teacher monitors the students and determines that they have written down as many answers as they can, the teacher places the students in the pair mode for further consultation. Switching to share mode, the pairs of students count their answers and challenge other pairs to see who has the most correct answers. The teacher may have pairs of students write their responses on the board. The teacher

should expect that some category may not be completed. If this is the case, see the suggested follow-up activity.

Individual Accountability:	Each student's paper may be collected by the teacher and marked as a completed activity (nongraded). This adds incentive to students who may not wish to do the activity.
Follow-Up:	If there is any category that does not have four answers for it, the teacher may have the students search in textbooks, encyclopedias, dictionaries, and other resources for additional terms. This activity can be done as a whole class or as individual homework assignments.

LANGUAGE ARTS

Preparing students for a Think-Pair-Share language arts lesson can be done while at the same time practicing the Think-Pair-Share strategy. A group builder such as Fall Colors can readily accomplish both goals.

ACTIVITY—FALL COLORS

Objective:	The Activity Sheet—Fall Colors (see Activity Sheet Appendix, Figure 8.5) pictures acorns, leaves, pumpkins, and squirrels. Pairs of students will color the pictures, cut them out, and arrange them.
Roles:	Pairs of students divide the pictures to color them. One student acts as the cutter to separate the pictures with scissors. The other student is the gluer, gluing the pictures down after the pairs of students have arranged the pictures.
Procedure:	Pairs of students are handed the picture handout. Together, the pair of students decides who will be the cutter and the gluer (think mode). The cutter cuts the handout into strips along the lines. Each student colors a column of pictures the color given at the top of the strip. After the pictures are colored, the cutter separates the pictures into piles (pair-mode problem solving).
	The students then arrange the individually separated pictures in the following way: Every row, column, and diagonal must

have a set of four different pictures in it. Thus, there will be one acorn, leaf, pumpkin, and squirrel per row, per column, and per diagonal. In addition, no color may be duplicated in any row, column, or diagonal.

When the students have arranged their picture squares into a four-by-four pattern, the gluer glues (think mode again) the picture squares to a blank piece of paper and posts it on the bulletin board for all to see (share mode). (Hint for the teacher: One way to solve this brain teaser is to place a different picture in each corner and then have the students arrange the remaining pictures.)

Follow-Up: The teacher may have students share orally with the class about how the pairs solved the puzzle. The students may be asked to write individually about the strategies used.

After using the group builder to practice Think-Pair-Share, students may move on to a more complex writing assignment. The writing lesson may be based upon a class novel, the reading textbook, or other reading materials selected by the teacher.

The Think-Pair-Share strategy can reduce time-consuming paperwork for the teacher. Instead of requiring each student to write out answers to comprehension questions that the teacher collects, reads, corrects, and grades, the teacher may use Think-Pair-Share. After the reading, the teacher states an oral comprehension question. The individual students think about an answer. Then the students meet with their partners and talk about ideas. Next, several of the pairs of students give their answers to the class. Students may add to, expand upon, and discuss the story as a class. Another approach is to have each student write out individual answers to comprehension questions. Then the pair switches papers to edit and revise its ideas. These papers may be collected by the teacher, or various ones may be shared with the class.

SCIENCE

To prepare students for a Think-Pair-Share lesson, use the group builder, What's for Lunch?

Content:	Scientific method, hypothesis testing
Objective:	Students will practice the scientific method by hypothesizing about what edible items are made from the lists of ingredients on the Activity Sheet—What's for Lunch?
Materials:	Activity Sheet—What's for Lunch? (see Activity Sheet Appendix, Figure 8.6)
Procedure:	The teacher explains that students will be practicing the scientific method by doing a fun activity called What's for Lunch? In the activity, they will hypothesize about edible products described by a list of ingredients only. First, they will attempt to name a product as individuals. Then they work in pairs to compare their thoughts. Finally, they will share their hypotheses with the class.
	This is an enjoyable activity because students make wild guesses and provide strange responses. When the actual products are named by the teacher, the students are often amazed at the big gap between their guesses and reality.
Answers:	(1) Strawberry yogurt, (2) vegetable soup, (3) dog food, (4) hot dog, (5) ketchup, (6) gelatin dessert, (7) fortune cookie, (8) chocolate candy, (9) vegetable juice.

ACTIVITY—Using the Sense of Smell

Objective:	Students will practice the use of the scientific method by using data from their senses.
Material:	The teacher can make laminated reusable charts for recording student names and guesses, and a bar graph chart for recording total observations.
Procedure:	The teacher provides an anticipatory setting for this lesson by spraying a scent or placing potpourri in the room while the students are outside of the classroom. The students begin talking about the scent upon re-entering the room. The teacher gives a brief overview of the forthcoming lesson, and allows the students to predict the number of scents that they will accu-

rately guess. The students record their guesses at the top of a ballot sheet.

The teacher places a ball of cotton into each of five film containers, adding to each ball one of these five scents: root beer, orange, banana, lemon, mint. The teacher directs each student to take out a piece of paper and number it from one to five. Each student smells each container, guesses what the smell is, and writes a name for the scent next to each number on the paper.

The teacher reads the guesses, and the students record the guesses on a chart. The chart has a place for each student's name and a list of the scents. The students record their ability to detect the correct scent by writing "yes" or "no" under each scent. The teacher reads the ballots to prevent cheating. An example appears below:

Student	Root Beer	Orange	Banana	Lemon	Mint
Name	Yes	No	No	Yes	Yes
Name	No	Yes	No	Yes	Yes

To encourage active participation, each student has a chart at his or her desk. As the teacher charts each student's results, the students also record the same data. Pairs of students check each other's work for accuracy. After the raw data is collected, a bar graph is made that shows the number of students who correctly detected each scent. In this manner, the students see graphically which odors are readily identified and which ones are more difficult to recognize.

The teacher explains to the students that they have used the scientific method to describe the sense of smell. Each student smelled a scent (collected data), decided what the scent was (hypothesized), wrote a guess on a piece of paper (recorded the data), listed the guess with other student's guesses (comparison of data), made a bar graph (data display), and discussed which scents were easy or difficult to detect (hypothesis testing). Concrete data has allowed the students to quickly attain knowledge through the scientific method.

Follow-Up: The scientific method can also be practiced using the other four senses.

Figure 8.7
PRACTICE PROBLEMS TO USE WITH YOUR CLASSES

If your students are to become proficient in problem solving, they will need to practice solving problems and discussing the solutions with others. Some sample problems follow.

1.   You are at home working on your homework assignment. You find you do not know how to solve the problems on the assignment.
2.   You are tired in the morning when you get to school.
3.   When you sit by a friend in class, your friend talks to you. You can't hear the teacher and are afraid you might get in trouble.
4.   You haven't been doing well on the weekly spelling test.
5.   A classmate calls your mother a name.

More Complex Problems

You can introduce factors that complicate the problem or limit the alternatives to encourage more advanced problem solving.

1.   A friend of yours tells you he/she is being beaten by his/her parents. She asks you what to do.
2.   You need help with part of your seatwork assignment. The teacher is working with another group of students and you are not allowed to disturb him/her.
3.   There is graffiti in the school bathroom. Your school has tried placing a monitor in the bathroom, but this has been ineffective. How would you solve the problem?
4.   You have several homework assignments that are due. Your parents are going to visit your aunt, and you must go with them. You are afraid you won't have time to do all the assignments.

(Activity appears here courtesy of Darcy Kraus, Topeka Public Schools, Topeka, Kansas.)

Upon completion of these two introductory approaches to the scientific method, students are ready for longer lessons related to the scientific method and problem-solving activities provided in science textbooks, manuals, or laboratories.

THE AFFECTIVE DOMAIN

Not all problem solving and critical thinking remains in the cognitive domain and focuses on academic achievement. Some problem solving can be in the affective domain, dealing with the emotional state of students and the personal problems that they face. The Think-Pair-Share strategy can be used successfully in the affective domain as well. Using Think-Pair-Share, the teacher assigns the following interpersonal problem-solving exercises.

CONCLUSION

Think-Pair-Share is an appropriate cooperative learning strategy for all subjects, skills, and grade levels. It clearly involves all of the students in their own learning. Indeed, it is an approach that guarantees maximum student involvement in the lesson.

SELECTED REFERENCES

Foyle, H. C., and Lyman, L. 1993. *The Interactive Classroom,* (videotape). Washington, D.C.: National Education Association.

Lyman, F. T. 1992. "Think-Pair-Share, Thinktrix, Thinklinks, and Weird Facts: An Interactive System for Cooperative Thinking." In *Enhancing Thinking Through Cooperative Learning,* edited by N. Davidson and T. Worsham. New York: Teachers College Press.

_____ 1993. *Think-Pair-Share,* (videotape). Washington, D.C.: National Education Association.

Chapter 9

CREATIVE THINKING

Something old, something new, something borrowed,
something blue. . . .
— *Traditional wedding rhyme*

Cooperative learning and creative thinking are natural companions. Cooperative learning and creative thinking are new ways of thinking about old patterns of education. Groups of people working together can use a cooperative learning strategy to enhance their creative thinking abilities. People trying to arrive at new solutions to problems can use creative thinking. These two methods enhance one another. Cooperative learning as a method and structure is a vehicle for the development of a skill, creative thinking.

If students are given a problem that calls for creative responses, they may attack it as a group by using the brainstorming techniques of Osborn (1963) and Parnes (1967). Within the cooperative learning structure, students use the brainstorming techniques of fluency, flexibility, categorization, originality, elaboration, and imagination to produce those creative solutions.

FLUENCY

Cooperative learning groups approach a problem through discussion and attempt to derive as many terms or solutions as possible. No idea is evaluated or eliminated at this stage. Every student has something to add to the group's list of ideas, and all ideas are treated equally and accepted equally. Unhindered by evaluation, creative and unusual concepts emerge to solve the problem. In addition, the nonevaluative process encourages maximum group involvement and individual feelings of self-worth.

Students can practice fluency by using the group-building activity entitled, Up. The teacher tells the groups of students to list as many words and phrases as they can that contain the word, *up,* such as *get up, sunup, upside-down,* and so on. (See Figure 9.1 for other possible answers.)

FIGURE 9.1
SOME POSSIBLE ANSWERS TO "UP ACTIVITY"

get up	sum up	ante up	step up
thumbs up	crack up	give up	stand up
sunny-side up	uptight	up-front	Up with People
up-and-coming	Batter up!	Seven-Up	Upland, California
Upton Sinclair	checkup	push-up	"Uptown Girl"
fold up	saddle up	fluff up	*Up the Down Staircase*
buckle up	wash up	turn up	make up
jump up	uppity	cuddle up	What's up, Doc?
chin-up	pickup truck	Ketchup	Pick-up Stix
going up	catch up	one up	foul up
to eat it up	hold up	pop up	sit-up
ups and downs	show up	open up	hands up
upstart	sunup	line up	hang up
tie up	upchuck	listen up	Up on the Roof
shut up	open up	throw up	upside down
lighten up	cheer up	spruce up	buck up

Another version of the same activity uses the word, *down.* See Figure 9.2 for suitable words or phrases that students might identify.

FIGURE 9.2
SOME POSSIBLE ANSWERS TO "DOWN ACTIVITY"

downtown	ups and downs	marked down
down on your luck	going down	breakdown
hand-me-down	down-home	downpour
down-in-the-heels	pipe down	downturn
downside	Churchhill Downs	Ease on down the road.
sundown	to look down your nose	fall down
down and dirty	slicked down	put-down
#10 Downing Street	Hugh Downs	Morton Downey, Jr.
Come on down!	Tear it down.	down-and-out

90

FLEXIBILITY

In the brainstorming stage, the cooperative learning group examines the completed list of terms or solutions (no matter how outrageous, obscure, or irrelevant they may be) and attempts to refashion or alter its list. The group may append and expand the list with new and varied ideas. The students take differing points of view (pros and cons) about items on their list in order to expand ideas and add them to the previous list.

CATEGORIZATION

Placing the listed terms into categories helps students visualize the many different types of answers generated by the group. If a category has few or no responses in it, the students can do more brainstorming to try to develop more items. One creative group-building activity that helps students practice categorization is called Spring. (activity countesy of Joanne Foyle, Emporia, Kansas). Groups of students are allowed to generate varied and multiple responses for the categories related to the letters that spell out the word *spring.*

ACTIVITY—SPRING

Objective:	Students brainstorm terms that fit into the listed categories prior to the discussion of categorization in a brainstorming activity.
Material:	Activity Sheet—Spring (see Activity Sheet Appendix, Figure 9.3)
Procedure:	In heterogeneous groups of three or four, students write down all the words they can think of that fall into one of five categories given on the activity sheet associated with the season of spring. Each item must start with one of the letters found in the word *spring.*
Individual Accountability:	Each student in the group must provide at least one idea per category. The idea must start with any of the six letters of *spring.*

Follow-Up: The teacher presents the need for brainstorming and the importance of categorizing the results of brainstorming. The teacher points out how the brainstormed ideas thus far are not in categories. Now that the students understand what a category is, the students can go back to their brainstormed lists and generate categories and place the ideas, terms, names, or solutions into categories. (See Activity Sheet Appendix, Figure 9-4.)

In categorizing, students are encouraged to create categories of solutions. For example, a learning group brainstorms solutions to one student's problem of not remembering to bring books back to school. Then members group the possible solutions into the categories listed in Figure 9-3 (see Activity Sheet Appendix).

ORIGINALITY

When the solution to a problem must be particularly creative, the student group examines the categorized solutions in order to originate or devise strategies that will work. In this stage, the more creative and unusual the response, the better. A way to determine the originality of a group's ideas is to ask other groups whether they came up with the same ideas. The teacher praises as original any ideas that only one group has listed.

International Symbols

To practice the three brainstorming techniques presented up to this point, students may use a simple brainstorming activity, International Symbols, as a creative group builder. The teacher introduces the concept of international signs, a concept that uses images, rather than words, to communicate. Examples of international signs are displayed, and the students are asked to think of as many different interpretations of the images as possible. Groups are complimented for *fluency* when they create the greatest number of ideas for each sign. Groups with creative and unusual ideas are praised for *originality* if they have listed interpretations not thought of by others. *Flexibility* is encouraged by asking the groups to brainstorm multiple answers to the question, "Why do we need international signs?" Groups who think of ideas that they can organize into the most categories (people reasons, money reasons, safety reasons) are also praised *(categorization)*.

As a related activity, students could design, create, and explain their own international signs.

Two more brainstorming techniques remain to be explored, elaboration and imagination.

ELABORATION

A key element of this brainstorming technique is for student groups to produce a tentative product or plan of action that will solve the problem posed by the teacher or other students. The detailed plan tells how the group would use the plan or create any products necessary to carry out the plan. The group has gone beyond brainstorming by looking at the more complex realities required to solve a problem.

IMAGINATION

At the apex of this process, the cooperative group envisions or makes predictions about how its solution would operate if actually put into effect.

Various problems can be dealt with in cooperative learning groups by using all of these brainstorming techniques imaginatively and creatively. Lyman and Foyle (1990) suggest using Group Builders to provide a positive and creative classroom environment that encourages creative thinking on the part of all students. In addition, other creative thinking approaches are documented in the Selected References at the end of this chapter.

A group builder that is useful to help students with imaginative ideas is Exaggeration.

ACTIVITY—EXAGGERATION

Objective: Students will write exaggerated sentences using given information.

Procedure:	The teacher shares a tall tale and has students discuss how exaggeration makes the story interesting. Each group receives the Activity Sheet—Exaggeration (see Activity Sheet Appendix, Figure 9.5), and tries to write as many creative exaggerations as it can. Exaggerations are then shared with the class.
Follow-Up:	Illustrations can be drawn with the exaggerated sentences as captions.

CONCLUSION

Cooperative learning moves student thinking beyond drill-and-practice activities that rehearse basic skills and knowledge. Wedding cooperative learning and creative thinking methodologies allows cooperative groups of students to generate original ideas. For elementary students this does not mean earthshaking, brand new, never-before-discovered learning, but it does mean, for them at their age, new and creative ways of thinking.

SELECTED REFERENCES

Adams, J. L. 1986. *The Care and Feeding of Ideas: A Guide to Encouraging Creativity.* Reading, Mass.: Addison-Wesley.

_____ 1986. *Conceptual Blockbusting: A Guide to Better Ideas.* Reading, Mass.: Addison-Wesley.

Bagley, M. T. 1987. *Using Imagery in Creative Problem Solving.* N.Y.: Trillium Press.

Baum, S. E., and Cray-Andrews, M. 1983. *Creativity 1, 2, 3.* N.Y.: Trillium Press.

Lyman, L. R., and Foyle, H. C. 1990. *Cooperative Grouping for Interactive Learning: Students, Teachers, and Administrators.* Washington, D.C.: National Education Association.

Osborn, A. F. 1963. *Applied Imagination,* 3rd ed. N.Y.: Scribner's.

Parnes, S. J. 1967. *Creative Behavior Workbook.* N.Y.: Scribner's.

Raudsepp, E. 1977. *Creative Growth Games.* N.Y.: Putnam.

Raudsepp, E. 1980. *More Creative Growth Games.* N.Y.: Putnam.

Raudsepp, E. 1987. *Growth Games for the Creative Manager.* N.Y.: Putnam.

Tegano, D. W., Moran, J. D., and Sawyers, J. K. 1991. *Creativity in Early Childhood Classrooms.* Washington, D.C.: National Education Association.

Torrance, E. P. 1977. *Creativity in the Classroom.* Washington, D.C.: National Education Association.

Torrance, E. P., and Myers, R. E. 1970. *Creative Learning and Teaching.* N.Y.: Dodd, Mead, and Company.

von Oech, R. 1983. *A Whack on the Side of the Head.* N.Y.: Warner Books.

_____ 1986. *A Kick in the Seat of the Pants.* N.Y.: Harper and Row.

Chapter 10

WHOLE LANGUAGE AND COOPERATIVE LEARNING

We must return to basics, but the "basics" of the 21st century are not only reading, writing, and arithmetic. They include communication and higher problem-solving skills, and scientific and technological literacy—the thinking tools that allow us to understand the technological world around us.
—Educating Americans for the 21st Century

Effective education in the 21st century calls for student acquisition of the basics, but it also calls for the integration of those basics into higher levels of skill attainment that can be developed through the use of whole language strategies. One of the most important purposes of schooling is to help students acquire skills to make them effective listeners, speakers, readers, and writers. Effective communication skills are necessary for success in school, in social relationships, and in job settings in later life. Communication skills are also an essential part of successful interaction in cooperative learning.

Whole language is a developmentally appropriate, child-centered, process-oriented, cross-curriculum approach to learning and teaching. Two assumptions about teaching and learning undergird the whole language philosophy. First, all children are assumed to be successful language learners as evidenced by their acquisition of oral language without direct instruction. Whole language teachers attempt to build on the child's learning success, moving the student on to even more effective levels of communication.

The second basic assumption of the whole language philosophy is that all language behavior moves from less sophisticated to more sophisticated levels of performance as human beings attempt to fulfill their social and communication needs. This assumption makes it necessary for students to work with others who possess more refined levels of language performance. Teachers are clearly in a position to model desired communication behaviors.

Cooperative learning is the ideal complement to whole language in the elementary classroom. The primary purpose of acquiring language skills is to communicate with others effectively. The basis of all cooperative learning interaction is language—students discuss ideas, resolve differences, and solve learning problems together through language. Cooperative interaction helps students to become better listeners and speakers. It invites them to discuss and appreciate literature and gives constant opportunities to improve writing skills.

When visiting a whole language classroom where cooperative learning is in use, one might observe the students using a basal reading series, literature text sets, self-selected pieces of children's literature, and a wide array of other resources for learning. Following are some of the resources especially appropriate for cooperative learning.

abstracts/digests	computer printouts	jokes/puns
advertisements	coupons	labels/logos
almanacs	dictionaries	licenses/diplomas
animal books	diaries/letters	magazines
anthologies	documents	maps/atlases
applications/contracts	epics	matchbooks
autobiographies	encyclopedias	menus
baseball cards	fables	microfilm
bibles	fairy tales	mysteries
biographies	family trees	myths
boxes/sacks/containers	fantasy	newspapers
brochures/pamphlets	ghost stories	nonfiction
bulletin boards	group projects	picture books
calendars	historical fiction	plays
captions/headlines	horoscopes	poems
cards	how-to books	puzzles/codes
cartoons/comics	indexes	receipts
certificates	instructions	recipes

reference books	short stories	thesauruses
romance novels	song lyrics	thriller stories
rules/regulations	sports	timetables
schedules	T-shirts/jackets	tickets
science fiction	tall tales	travel guides
scripts	textbooks	westerns

An ever-changing menu of reading materials makes language arts instruction more meaningful and interesting to students.

In addition to the written resources available for cooperative learning activities in whole language, the teacher can also vary instruction by using a diversity of visual and auditory resources. These include:

audiotapes	charts	diagrams
films/filmstrips	graphs/tables	interactive video
movies	photographs	pictures/drawings
radio	records	slides
television	videotapes	

This smorgasbord of written, visual, and auditory resources is available not only for instruction but also to cooperative groups as they look for information and present it to other students.

The teacher and the other students in the classroom are not the only human resources used for learning about language. Other teachers, paraprofessionals, parents, or community members may serve as instructors or facilitators. Following are a few more possible human resources for whole language learning.

other teachers	other school personnel	parents
younger students	older students	senior citizens
community leaders	college students	

For example, students can work in cooperative groups to make books for younger students in the school. Older students and senior citizens can serve as tutors for groups and individuals who are having difficulty with certain skills. Students can write pen-pal letters to senior citizens in nursing homes. Students can interview community members in order to build an oral history of the community. Cooperation in groups naturally leads to relationships beyond the walls of the classroom.

Cooperative learning can provide motivation for students to acquire language skills. Successful group interaction requires each group member to be an effective listener and speaker. In order to work together on assignments and projects, group members must also become good readers and writers.

Evaluation of whole language may occur through observations of the process or the product of the cooperative groups, checklists, interviews, conferences, or individual tests. Thematic units may be used to demonstrate connections between reading, writing, speaking, listening, and other subject areas.

LISTENING SKILLS

Listening is an important social skill that students need to acquire to cooperate with others in the classroom and in later life. It is also a practical communication skill that should be a part of the language arts curriculum.

Listening is done on different levels. At the most basic level, the student can accurately repeat the message of the speaker, as in paraphrasing a previous student's response. More advanced listening skills require the student to evaluate factors such as tone of voice and nonverbal communication (e.g., angry vocal tones, friendly body posture) to understand the context and meaning of the message. When the listener demonstrates empathy for the speaker, the speaker is encouraged to relax and to communicate more information and feelings.

Cooperative learning can provide opportunities to practice needed listening skills in nonthreatening and fun ways. In the following activity, students practice changing the meaning of simple phrases by using different tones of voice.

ACTIVITY—TONE OF VOICE

Objective: Students will observe how different tones of voice can change the meaning of a simple phrase.

Procedure: The teacher shows how tone of voice can change the meaning of a phrase by saying the following sentence sincerely: "I really like the way you did your homework last night!" Then the teacher changes the meaning of the phrase by using a different tone, such as a sarcastic tone.

Students brainstorm other tones that can change meaning, such as anger, questioning, uncertainty.

Students are grouped in pairs. The teacher has written phrases such as the following on individual slips of paper. Each pair draws a phrase from the following list.

"I'd love to go."

"That sounds like a lot of fun."

"Oh, Mother!"

"I really like my new teacher."

"I'm sure he's telling the truth."

"I think homework is a good idea."

"The lunch today was delicious."

"The book we're reading is very interesting."

The pairs practice saying the phrase so that it takes on a literal meaning. Then they think of at least one way to change the meaning by using a different tone of voice.

Two pairs are then grouped together. Each pair shares its phrase and the ways they have thought of to change the meaning. The other pair decides when the phrase actually means what it says.

Follow-Up: Students think of facial expressions and postures that can change the meaning of expressions. Using the preceding list, pairs practice changing the meaning by altering nonverbal behaviors.

RESPONDING TO LITERATURE

Student appreciation for literature can be enhanced by discussing literature together in cooperative groups. Such discussions build interest and enhance understanding as students relate personal experiences, exchange points of view, and make decisions about the meaning of literary works.

There are many strategies for grouping students to discuss literature. Groups can be assigned to read different literary resources about the same topic and to share information about their resource with the class. In addition, the class can read or listen to the same literary source and discuss the source in groups in response to questions generated by the class or by the teacher.

In the following activity, the teacher reads part of a book to the students. Working in cooperative groups, the students discuss teacher-prepared questions about the reading.

ACTIVITY—COOPERATIVE DISCUSSION OF LITERATURE

Objective: Students will cooperatively discuss a passage from *A Wrinkle in Time* and think of ways to help students who are having trouble in school.

Procedure: The teacher reads pages 5, 6, 30, and 31 from *A Wrinkle in Time* (Scholastic) to the class. In this story, the main character, Meg Murry, is having difficulty in school work and peer relationships because she is growing up and because conditions in her family are unsettled due to her father's absence.

Students are grouped in heterogeneous groups of three or four. Each group is given a list of discussion questions about the reading (see Activity Sheet Appendix—Questions on *A Wrinkle in Time*, Figure 10.1).

When the groups are finished, the teacher asks each group to share some of their ideas. The groups' papers may be collected and commented on in writing by the teacher to provide feedback to the group.

If the teacher wants an individual grade for this activity, each student can be asked to respond to the question: "What could you do to help Meg if she were a student in our class?"

Students who are interested in or concerned about a particular topic can be grouped together to read a book about the topic and discuss it together. New insights can be gained, and support from other students who share a common interest or problem can result from these cooperative discussions. Following is a list of appropriate books related to timely student topics.

Bullies:

Byars, Betsy, *The 18th Emergency*, Avon.
Carson, Nancy, *Loudmouth George and the Sixth Grade Bully*, Carolrhoda.
Stolz, Mary, *The Bully of Barkham Street*, Harper and Row.

Death:

Boyd, Candy, *Breadsticks and Blessing Places*, Macmillan.
Paterson, Katherine, *Bridge to Terebithia*, Crowell.
Smith, Doris, *A Taste of Blackberries*, Scholastic.
Taylor, Theodore, *The Cay*, Avon Camelot. (Also relates to prejudice.)

Divorce:

Cleary, Beverly, *Dear Mr. Henshaw*, Dell.
Gary, Paulsen, *Hatchet*, Puffin.
Hobbs, Will, *Changes in Latitude*, Atheneum.
Mann, Peggy, *My Dad Lives in a Downtown Hotel*, Scholastic.
Rylant, Cynthia, *But I'll Be Back Again*, Orchard Books.
Sachs, Marilyn, *Veronica Ganz*, Archway.

Families:

Adoff, Arnold, *Black is Brown is Tan*, Harper and Row.
Campbell, Hope, *Why Not Join the Giraffes?*, Dell.
Hamilton, Virginia, *Cousins*, Apple.
Tax, Meredith, *Families*, Little Brown.

Foster Children:

Byars, Betsy, *The Pinballs,* Scholastic.
Carlson, Natalie, *Ann Aurelia and Dorothy,* Harper and Row.
Paterson, Katherine, *The Great Gilly Hopkins,* Crowell.

Prejudice:

Edell, Celeste, *A Present from Rosita,* Archway.
Friedman, Frieda, *A Sundae with Judy,* Scholastic.
Jackson, Jesse, *Call Me Charley,* Dell.
Taylor, Mildred, *Mississippi Bridge,* Bantam-Skylark.

Sibling Conflict:

Blume, Judy, *Tales of a Fourth Grade Nothing,* Dell.
Byars, Betsy, *The Summer of the Swans,* Viking.
Cleary, Beverly, *Ramona the Pest,* William Morrow.
Lowry, Lois, *Anastasia Krupnik,* Bantam-Skylark.

Homelessness:

Bunting, Eve, *I'll Fly Away,* Clarion.
Spinelli, Jerry, *Maniac Magee,* Harper Trophy.
Warner, Gertrude Chandler, *Boxcar Children,* Scholastic.

WRITING AND READING WORKSHOPS

The writing or reading workshop is a good way to structure cooperative language activities (Atwell 1987). This approach stresses problem solving, individual accountability, responsibility, and the need to cooperate with other students. There are four main components of the writing or reading workshop: (1) writing or reading, (2) instruction, (3) conferencing, and (4) sharing.

In the *writing workshop,* students have daily opportunities to *write* on self-selected topics in journals, learning logs, and in projects in all areas of the curriculum.

Instruction is provided to introduce authors, to explore modes of writing and genre, and to learn strategies for improving writing. Specific strategies, such as the Six Traits Model (Spandel and Stiggins 1990), identified by the Northwest Regional Laboratory, can be taught to students so that they can assess strengths and weaknesses in their own writing and that of their peers. Students may work together in cooperative groups to collaborate on writing projects, co-author and illustrate books, share works in progress, celebrate completed works, or practice a strategy.

Conferences about the students' writing take place in many forms and for a variety of purposes. Teachers and individual students may conference about topic selection, about progress on drafts, or about editing in preparation for publishing. Students may also conference with each other in pairs or writers' groups to discuss similar topics.

Conferencing in pairs or in writers' groups provides opportunities for students to practice and refine language skills. Listening skills develop as group members listen for specific criteria within a draft of one of the members. The writer must refine speaking skills as he or she outlines precisely what group members are to listen for and what type of help is wanted. For example, the writer may ask group members to identify strengths or weaknesses in the draft or to listen for overused words. Reading skills develop as group members read each other's drafts and rate ideas, organization, sentence fluency, word choice, or conventions. Writing skills improve as group members' suggestions are incorporated into the draft.

Sharing can occur in whole class groups or in smaller cooperative groups. Again, all modes of language are practiced as the writer reads a piece of writing. Listeners must listen carefully so that they can tell the writer what specific things they liked about the writing, to ask questions about parts of the writing that were unclear, or to ask for more details and information.

The *reading workshop* follows a pattern similar to the writing workshop. *Instruction* is provided to teach skills and model strategies. Students *read* daily, either materials that are self-selected or selected by cooperative groups. *Conferences* are conducted between individual students and the teacher to check progress. *Sharing* of the book or books read by each group takes place in small groups or whole class sharing times.

GROUP ROLES

Group roles can help all group members participate when they share with the class. One way to assign roles is to hand out the activity sheet in Figure 10.2 (see Activity Sheet Appendix) and allow group members to choose the role or roles they will play. Whether students select or are assigned roles, the teacher gains the option of grading the individual's product while rewarding the group as a whole in some other way.

BUILDING AN EXPERIENCE-BASED THEMATIC UNIT

Experience-based thematic units build on an experience that was shared by the whole class together. Storytelling provides an ideal vehicle for constructing an experience-based thematic unit.

Storytelling is an additive; it expands lesson plans to proportions much larger then the story itself. Storytelling is flexible and can be easily adapted for use in the classroom. The story of "The Gingerbread Boy" may be too simple for older elementary classrooms, but any basic story, folktale, myth, or fable that is interesting to students will serve. The teacher makes the story the unifying feature in a unit of diverse activities. For example, with a story such as "The Gingerbread Boy," the student is assigned to measure ingredients and bake gingerbread. Here are activities from a gingerbread boy unit that can be adapted to other stories and to various grade levels.

1. Apply math skills to the manipulation of amounts of ingredients.
2. Write a new ending for the story to develop writing skills.
3. Select and study specific words for the weekly spelling test.
4. Create a real gingerbread boy from actual ingredients supplied by the instructor.
5. Analyze the ingredients according to the four basic food groups for nutritional awareness.

6. Research the mountain region that serves as the setting for the story.
7. Test students' memory to develop listening skills.
8. Learn to outline the main points of the story.
9. Adjust the story to fit all four seasons.
10. Change the location of the story to a busy city.
11. Interview family members for favorite foods.
12. Write to the manufacturer for information about the processing of modern foods.
13. Tour a production plant.
14. Research similar stories in the library.
15. Portray the story in a class play.
16. Make a map of the actual route taken by the Gingerbread Boy.
17. Apply the moral of the story to their own lives.
18. Illustrate parts of the story.
19. Analyze the development of the plot.
20. Identify the adjectives, nouns, and other parts of speech in the story.
21. Create metaphors from the story.
22. Identify colors of the setting.

Storytelling can also be used to develop topical thematic units. If the teacher is focusing on Australia, it is probable that one of the many Australian folktales will assist the students in writing, listening, vocabulary identification, oral communication, and so on. Storytelling is a craft that serves the teacher in any format.

(Gingerbread Boy activities contributed by Denny Dey, Benedictine College, Atchison, Kansas.)

CONCLUSION

Successful social interaction depends on students who are skilled speakers, listeners, writers, and readers. The exchange of ideas that takes place in cooperative learning groups is essential to a whole language classroom that focuses on the acquisition of these important skills by using a variety of resources. Cooperative learning is an ideal vehicle for practicing language arts skills and for helping students become more successful communicators.

SELECTED REFERENCES

Atwell, N. 1987. *In the Middle: Writing, Reading, and Learning with Adolescents.* Portsmouth, N.H.: Boynton/Cook.

Baskwill, J., and Whitman, P. 1988. *Evaluation: Whole Language, Whole Child.* Jefferson City, Mo.: Scholastic.

Cihak, M. K., and Jackson, B. H. 1980. *Games Children Should Play: Sequential Lessons for Teaching Communication Skills in Grades K-6.* Glenview, Ill.: Scott Foresman.

Egan, K. 1986. *Teaching as Storytelling.* Chicago: University of Chicago Press.

Graves, L. N., and Graves, T. (eds.). 1991. Cooperative Learning and Language Arts (Theme issue). *Cooperative Learning: The Magazine for Cooperation in Education* 11(4).

Heath, S. B. , and Mangiola, L. 1991. *Children of Promise: Literate Activity in Linguistically and Culturally Diverse Classrooms.* Washington, D.C.: National Education Association.

Manning, M., and Manning, G. (eds). 1989. *Whole Language: Beliefs and Practices, K-8.* Washington, D.C.: National Education Association.

Spandel, V., and Stiggins, R. 1990. *Creating Writers.* N.Y.: Addison-Wesley.

Stone, J. M. 1989. *Cooperative Learning and Language Arts: A Multi-Structural Approach.* San Juan Capistrano, Calif.: Resources for Teachers.

Chapter 11

ASSESSING COOPERATIVE LEARNING THROUGH PORTFOLIOS

> *There is no "right" way to implement portfolios. The most important idea is the spirit of portfolios: developing class-room practices and traditions that reflect a student-centered approach to assessment.*
>
> —*Tierney, Carter, and Desai*

Portfolios are purposeful gatherings of products to demonstrate student performance. They are an assessment strategy that documents both the goals of instruction and the student's progress toward those goals. Their appearance and format vary widely because they serve different purposes.

An important part of cooperative learning is reflection on the achievement of the original goal, the process used, and the final product. An appropriate means of assessing cooperative learning is through the use of portfolios.

Portfolio assessment is the natural ally of teachers who believe in child-centered process approaches to learning because authentic classroom work is used to demonstrate student growth. Emphasis is on strengths, improvement, development and control of skills, personal preferences, and appreciations. These provide a broader picture of a student's achievement by showing the unfolding of skills over time, rather than a one-time performance on a standardized test.

Students and parents, along with teachers, are often involved in the development and evaluation of portfolios. Together, they determine the purposes, the contents, and the method(s) of evaluation. All parties may contribute reflection sheets to the portfolios. In some portfolios, items from home are included to round out the picture of the student.

Teachers can communicate clearly what is valued and can integrate instruction and assessment. All interested parties become allies in assessment. Motivation is enhanced as effort, collaboration, reflection, exploration, understanding, application, and revision are rewarded rather than only correct answers. As students take partial responsibility and control for their own learning, they begin to develop internally-imposed standards and move beyond minimum competencies.

PURPOSES OF PORTFOLIOS

The contents of each portfolio are determined by the purpose, audience, and time frame of the portfolio. The *classroom unit portfolio* is addressed to the teacher, and its purpose is to assign a grade. This portfolio might cover a two- to four-week period and include a list of materials read, drawings of various habitats, a written report with all drafts attached, a photograph of a bulletin board, an audiotape of a song written about habitats, a copy of a letter requesting information written to a wildlife agency, and a teacher-made test covering the material. The classroom unit portfolio can also include all the drafts, finished products, evaluation criteria, and reflection forms used in a curriculum unit such as one on animal habitats.

A second type of portfolio can demonstrate the achievement of goals related to specific *student competencies*. It is reviewed by parents, the principal, the student, and next year's teacher. Decisions about promotion or class placement might be made by using this portfolio. Contents often include a writing sample with all drafts, an audiotape of oral reading done monthly during the year, photographs of science and social studies projects, a math learning-log, and work on written story problems. In addition, a curriculum-related competency checklist as well as norm-referenced and criterion-referenced test results would be appropriate in this portfolio.

A third portfolio to document the achievement of outcomes for a *state assessment* might include best pieces from several prescribed curriculum areas. A norm-referenced or criterion-referenced test might also be included. The audience is raters/auditors from the state who do not know the student or the teacher. Contents for such portfolios often must follow strict guidelines.

A fourth type of portfolio, the *showcase portfolio,* is developed to celebrate student achievement over an extended time period: the school year, the elementary school years, the school career from kindergarten through high school graduation. This portfolio often contains samples of best work. Audiences for such portfolios also vary. Some may be used for college admission or for employment. Other uses of showcase portfolios allow parents to review samples of work from each year in school to document growth and achievement.

CONTENTS OF A PORTFOLIO

Because the purposes and audiences of portfolios vary so widely, there is no standard format. Some portfolios are simply a file folder, while others are accordion folders or small boxes. As technology improves, portfolios recorded on microfilm, computer disks, or laser disks will be common.

Because portfolios strive to present a well-rounded picture of the student, many different types of material are included. Anthony, Johnson, Mickelson, and Preece (1991) recommend that data be gathered from four sources: observation of the process, observation of the children's products, classroom measures, and decontextualized measures (see Data Gathering—A Classroom Approach, Figure 11.1). For further discussion of these ideas see the researchers' book, *Evaluating Literacy: A Perspective for Change.*

At the front of the portfolio, a table of contents or organizational chart helps the audience interpret the contents. Such introductory material should also include a description of the purpose, contents, and audience for which the portfolio was designed. Lists of requirements and evaluation criteria are also appropriate and helpful.

To maximize student involvement and learning, each piece included should have a form used by the student to reflect on and evaluate each piece included. Such forms often ask the student to answer the following questions.

FIGURE 11.1

DATA GATHERING—A CLASSROOM APPROACH

Anecdotal comments from
classroom observation
and reflection

Interviews/conferences:
student, parents, and
other professionals

Responses to reading:
retelling, text
reconstruction

Reading logs
Learning logs
Selected pages from
notebooks or journals
Audiotapes
Pupil self-assessments
Writing folders
Interest inventories

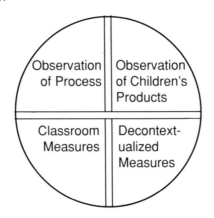

Observation
of Process

Observation
of Children's
Products

Classroom
Measures

Decontext-
ualized
Measures

Text-related activities
Teacher-made unit
(content-concept) tests

Criterion-referenced
measures
District or cross-grade
examinations
Provincial or state
examinations

- Why was this piece selected?
- What are its best features?
- What does this piece demonstrate about my learning?
- If I had more time, what would I do differently about this piece?

For some portfolios, students are asked to include items from outside of school that help to complete a picture of their growth as a learner.

USING PORTFOLIOS IN COOPERATIVE LEARNING ACTIVITIES

Portfolios similar to the one described for use in a unit of study can be used for cooperative learning activities, especially when such activities extend over several days. Students might include records of the tasks/roles assigned to each group member and how and when such tasks/roles were completed. Audiotapes of group interactions can be included. Final products along with drafts, schematics, and preliminary plans could be included. For three-dimensional objects or large objects, photographs rather than the actual object could be substituted for the product.

An important part of cooperative learning is reflection on the achievement of the original goal/outcome, the process used, and the final product. The Group Assessment/Project Evaluation Form in Figure 11.2 can be completed by each group member.

The first of the final two questions ("Were there members of your group who made exceptional contributions? Who?") is included to gauge each member's ability to recognize and celebrate the contributions of other group members. The second question ("Were there members of your group who did not pull their weight? Who?") elicits information that (1) evaluates the achievement of cooperative learning goals, (2) shows the student's ability to recognize the differing ways in which group members contribute to group success, and (3) indicates that true collaboration and group effort exist. In a well-functioning cooperative group, students will list names under the first of the

Figure 11.2
Group Assessment/Project Evaluation Form

Self-Evaluation

Directions: Rate yourself in relation to your performance on the assessment project by using the following scale.

Excellent = 5   Good = 4   Fair = 3   Poor = 2   No Contribution = 1

I was prepared to contribute to the group.	
(I read the assigned material.)	5 4 3 2 1
I contributed my ideas.	5 4 3 2 1
I asked others for their ideas.	5 4 3 2 1
I encouraged others to participate in the group.	5 4 3 2 1
I stayed on task.	5 4 3 2 1
I helped others stay on task.	5 4 3 2 1
I did my fair share of the work.	5 4 3 2 1
Overall, I feel my performance in the group should	
be rated:	5 4 3 2 1

Group Evaluation

Directions: Rate your group in relation to the assessment project by using the following scale.

Excellent = 5   Good = 4   Fair = 3   Poor = 2   No Contribution = 1

Our group was task-oriented.	5 4 3 2 1
Everyone was prepared by reading	
assigned materials.	5 4 3 2 1
Everyone's ideas were respected.	5 4 3 2 1
The quality of our presentation can be described as:	5 4 3 2 1
The quality of our handouts can be described as:	5 4 3 2 1

Were there members of your group who made *exceptional* contributions? Who?

_____   _____

_____   _____

Were there members of your group who did not "pull their weight"? Who?

_____   _____

_____   _____

two questions and will list no names under the second question or will make a statement such as, "No, I think we worked together well," or "We all contributed equally."

Rubrics that establish criteria for evaluation are useful in helping students rate and evaluate their performance. The Six-Trait Analytical Model (1990) is one such rubric for use on written products. By using such a rubric, students can evaluate their own performance on a cooperative learning project.

Following are two examples of cooperative learning activities that are accompanied by self-evaluation rubrics or teacher evaluation forms.

PORTFOLIO ACTIVITY—ADVERTISING PICTURE BOOK

Content Area: Social studies/language arts/advertising strategies

Objective: Students will produce a picture book that demonstrates different advertising strategies used by advertisers to sell their products.

Procedure: After completing the activity "Advertising Strategies" in Chapter 6 of this book, students will develop a picture book that clearly identifies at least six strategies used by advertisers.

In general, it is good to give as few directions as possible to the group. However, students will appreciate a few ideas from numerous nonfiction picture books on a wide variety of related topics. Three excellent resources that suggest publishing ideas are *How to Make Books with Children*, Volume I and II, by Joy Evans and Jo Ellen Moore; *Making Big Books with Children*, by Joy Evans, Kathleen Morgan, and Jo Ellen Moore; and *Writing: Teachers and Children at Work*, by Donald Graves. The Figure 11.3 Activity Sheet also might be used. (See Activity Sheet Appendix.) Figure 11.4 goes with the Activity Sheet.

ACTIVITY—JIGSAW COOPERATIVE LEARNING

Content Area: This activity is designed for any content that can be learned through reading and discussion.

FIGURE 11.4
ADVERTISING PICTURE BOOK EVALUATION FORM

Name _____

__30__ *Clarity of Concept Presentation*
_____ 1. The picture book clearly conveys an understanding of the topic.
_____ 2. The picture book conveys a surface understanding of the topic.
_____ 3. The picture book does not clearly convey an understanding of the topic.

__30__ *Information Accuracy*
_____ 1. All of the information is accurately presented.
_____ 2. Most of the information is accurately presented.
_____ 3. Little of the information is accurately presented.

__10__ *Information is Presented Visually and in Words*
_____ 1. Both images and words work together to bring about understanding of the material.
_____ 2. Both words and images are used, but do not work together well to present a coherent message.
_____ 3. Both words and pictures are not used.

__10__ *Originality, Creativity, and/or Risk Taking*
_____ 1. The picture book demonstrates evidence of thought and problem solving.
_____ 2. The picture book demonstrates evidence of presenting the information in a very academic way.
_____ 3. The picture book does not meet the requirements of the assignment.

__10__ *Product Quality*
_____ 1. The mechanics and construction are of professional quality.
_____ 2. The book contains some mechanical errors and/or the physical construction of the book is not of professional quality.
_____ 3. The book contains many mechanical errors and/or the book is shabbily constructed.

__30__ *Completion of the "Reflection on the Product" Form*
_____ 1. The form is completed and shows evidence of productive reflection.
_____ 2. The form is completed, but responses are only surface comments.
_____ 3. The form is not completed.

Total Points
_____/100

Objective:	Students will learn through reading and discussion in cooperative groups. They will not only demonstrate their mastery of the material by taking a quiz; they will also complete a thoughtful evaluation of the group process and their role in it.
Procedure:	Jigsaw II (Slavin 1991) places students into groups to read parts of a chapter, article, or text, or to read different materials dealing with a similar topic. The students are given Activity Sheet—Jigsaw Cooperative Learning Assignment (see Activity Sheet Appendix, Figure 11.5), which tells each student which material he or she is responsible for.
	The students bring their sources and 10 important ideas on the topic to their cooperative group for discussion. Then students meet with "expert" groups—students from other teams who have read the same material. After discussion within the expert groups, students return to their original teams to teach their portion of the material to their group mates. Questions about the material can be provided to the original teams and/or the expert groups.
Accountability:	Assessment of learning is done on an individual basis (by test or quiz) to ensure individual accountability.
	As an assessment of group learning, the teacher conducts a Jigsaw cooperative learning activity with the cooperative groups (see Figure 11.5).

A form similar to the one in Figure 11.6 can be completed for each student individually and made a part of the portfolio.

FIGURE 11.6
INDIVIDUAL EVALUATION FORM

Name_____   Group_____

_____ 0-20 points   Preparation of the one-page listing 10 major points from material read
_____ 0-20 points Individual score on the test/quiz
_____ 0-20 points Average score of the group on the test/quiz
_____ 0-20 points Thoughtful completion of the Self/Group Evaluation
_____ Total points (80 possible)

CONCLUSION

There are a variety of assessment approaches that are specific to each individual cooperative learning strategy. However, the use of portfolio assessment appears to be an appropriate general tool to use with all cooperative learning approaches.

SELECTED REFERENCES

Anthony, R. J., Johnson, T. D., Mickelson, N. I., and Preece, A. 1991. *Evaluating Literacy: A Perspective for Change.* Portsmouth, N.H.: Heinemann.

Dalheim, M. (ed.) 1993. *Student Portfolios.* Washington, D.C.: National Education Association.

De Fina, A. A. 1992. *Portfolio Assessment: Getting Started.* N.Y.: Scholastic.

Evans, J., and Moore, J. E. 1985. *How to Make Books with Children.* Monterey, Calif.: Evan-Moor.

Evans, J., Morgan, K., and Moore, J. E. 1987. *Making Big Books with Children.* Monterey, Calif.: Evan-Moor.

Graves, Donald. 1983. *Writing: Teachers and Children at Work.* Portsmouth, N.H.: Heinemann.

Graves, L. N., and Graves, T. 1992. Assessment in Cooperative Learning (Thematic Issue). *Cooperative Learning: The Magazine for Cooperation in Education* 13(1).

Herman, J. L., Aschbacher, P. R., and Winters, L. 1992. *A Practical Guide to Alternative Assessment.* Alexandria, Va.: Association for Supervision and Curriculum Development.

Slavin, R.E. 1991. *Using Student Team Learning,* 3rd edition. Baltimore, Md.: The Johns Hopkins Team Learning Project, Center for Research on Elementary and Middle Schools, Johns Hopkins University.

Spandel, V., and Stiggins, R. 1990. *Creating Writers.* N.Y.: Addison-Wesley.

Tierney, R. J., Carter, M. A., and Desai, L. E. 1991. *Portfolio Assessment in the Reading-Writing Classroom.* Norwood, Mass.: Christopher-Gordon.

INITIAL USE OF COOPERATIVE LEARNING

> *The mere formulation of a problem is often far more es-*
> *sential than its solution, which may be merely a matter*
> *of mathematical or experimental skill. To raise new ques-*
> *tions, new possibilities; to regard old problems from a*
> *new angle, requires creative imagination and marks real*
> *advances in science.*
>
> *—Albert Einstein*

There will be problems in any methodology that a teacher chooses to use with students. As Einstein indicated, working out a problem is not merely applying a skill in a rote manner; it requires some creative thinking and different ways of looking at situations. Cooperative learning is a way of changing a classroom environment. It provides a different way of examining classroom management, discipline, grading, and relationships with students.

Recall the Gilda Radner character, Emily Litella, on the original *Saturday Night Live* television show. She mistook something she heard "conserving our natural resources" for "conserving our national racehorses." She proceeded to deliver a long editorial harangue about the issue. When she was corrected about what she had heard, she shrugged: "Never mind."

Classroom teachers cannot say "never mind." They have to deal with problems as they arise. And they will arise when any innovation is adopted for classroom use. For this reason, the authors recommend preparation, even for the negatives. Teachers need to be aware of specific problems that can develop when using cooperative learning. Some basic cautions and helpful hints can get teachers off to a solid start and accentuate the positives.

A common worry of higher achieving students is that they will be expected to do all the work of a group. Indeed, parents of higher achieving students may believe that a group grade given to all members of a group is a direct result of their student's individual work. A clear explanation of the teaching methodology to students, parents, and administrators alleviates some of these problems.

The classroom teacher who uses cooperative learning must be ready to explain the methodology's purposes and benefits; social and academic goals and objectives; and the specific strategy used to practice the skills, concepts, and desired learning. Teachers must point out that individual effort of each student *is* important and that individual work will be assessed and graded.

Advance preparation can prevent some of the misunderstandings that occur within cooperative groups. Lyman and Foyle (1990) provide group-building activities that help promote a positive small group and classroom environment. This sets the pattern for wholesome small group discussion and helps to overcome misunderstandings, both verbal and nonverbal.

As groups are functioning, the teacher can nip many potential problems in the bud. He or she circulates from group to group around the room looking for positive progress and alert to any negative comments or actions. As these occur, a simple and timely response by the teacher on a one-to-one basis can deter larger problems. In any event, clear instructions, direct guidance and demonstrations, constant checking for understanding, and giving appropriate feedback to students can solve numerous classroom problems.

TROUBLESHOOTING FOR COOPERATIVE LEARNING

Some proven troubleshooting hints for teachers who are initiating cooperative learning are presented in the list that follows. Teachers may also share observed positive examples of group dialog as models for other groups to use.

- State your lesson objective clearly and make sure that cooperative learning is an appropriate strategy for that objective.
- Avoid overusing cooperative learning. Use other strategies as well.
- Avoid group grading. If rewards are to be used, make the rewards "add-ons" or bonuses that all groups can earn if they work well together.

- Make sure students clearly understand the purpose for new classroom activities and procedures such as cooperative learning.
- Teach the skills needed for working together in groups.
- Be especially sure that directions are clear to students. Model a desired behavior or skill yourself or have students model it before beginning individual or small group work. Doublecheck for understanding by having students repeat the directions back to you.
- Monitor by walking around and observing individuals and groups while they are working.
- After cooperative activities, provide the opportunity for group process to identify what went well and what can be improved next time.
- Discuss situations that upset individual students, or deal with the situation in small groups, as appropriate. Students' nonverbal behavior will sometimes indicate they are upset even if they don't say anything.
- Use group-building activities to help students get acquainted and build trust in the classroom.

Implementation of any new learning approach creates questions and raises anxieties among students, parents, and administrators. Such potentially negative reactions can be avoided or minimized, but the best defense is a good offense. Build cooperative learning on a sound foundation, making sure each activity succeeds. The following guidelines help accomplish that success.

INITIATING COOPERATIVE LEARNING

1. Inform your administrator that you are using cooperative learning methods. Be ready to explain your goals, expected outcomes, and the research benefits of cooperative learning.
2. Inform parents that you are using cooperative learning. The NEA pamphlet, *Cooperative Learning: What You Need to Know (1991),* may help parents understand cooperative learning better.
3. Teach group processes to students. Don't expect your students to already have the skills needed to work successfully in groups.

4. Start slowly. Use cooperative learning sparingly until you are confident with it and sure that it is working for your class.
5. Create a classroom atmosphere that encourages cooperative learning. Encourage student ownership, active participation, high expectations, and positive feelings. These are the foundation for cooperative learning and successful classroom management.
6. Promote student success. Ensure that early experiences with cooperative learning are highly successful and rewarding for students.
7. Monitor student reactions and conference individually to reassure students who are troubled by cooperative learning. High-achieving students sometimes need this reassurance.
8. Monitor the effectiveness of your teaching. Use the same individual evaluation procedures you normally use. You may also wish to monitor student achievement, attitudes, attendance, discipline referrals, and behavior outside of the classroom as indicators of the success of your methods.
9. Network with other teachers. Join or form a support group of other teachers who also use cooperative learning for problem solving, celebration, and exchanging ideas.

Prior to implementing cooperative learning, classroom teachers should realize that no harm can come to students through the appropriate implementation of cooperative learning strategies. The benefits of cooperative learning are well established and should be a part of any elementary teacher's repertoire.

SELECTED REFERENCES

Foyle, H. C., and Lyman, L. 1991. *Cooperative Learning: What You Need to Know* (pamphlet). Washington, D.C.: National Education Association.

Lyman, L. 1990. "Dealing with Misunderstanding in the Cooperative Classroom." *Kansas ASCD Record* 8(4), 1–3.

Lyman, L., and Foyle, H. C. 1990. *Cooperative Grouping for Interactive Learning: Students, Teachers, and Administrators.* Washington, D.C.: National Education Association.

BIBLIOGRAPHY

Albert, L. 1989. *Cooperative Discipline: How to Manage Your Classroom and Promote Self-Esteem.* Circle Pines, Minn.: American Guidance Service.

Bennett, B., Rolheiser-Bennett, C., and Stevahn, L. 1991. *Cooperative Learning: Where Heart Meets Mind.* Toronto, Canada: Educational Connections.

Brubacher, M., Payne, R., and Rickett, K., eds. 1990. *Perspectives on Small Group Learning: Theory and Practice.* Oakville, Ontario, Canada: Rubicon Publishing.

Clarke, J., Wideman, R., and Eadie, S. 1990. *Together We Learn.* Scarborough, Ontario, Canada: Prentice-Hall.

Cohen, E. 1986. *Designing Groupwork: Strategies for the Heterogeneous Classroom.* New York: Teacher's College Press.

Davidson, N., ed. 1989. *Cooperative Learning in Mathematics: A Handbook for Teachers.* Reading, Mass.: Addison-Wesley.

Davidson, N., and Worsham, T., eds. 1992. *Enhancing Thinking Through Cooperative Learning.* New York: Teachers College Press.

DeVries, D., Slavin, R., Gennessey, G., Edwards, K., and Lombardo, N. 1980. *Teams-Games-Tournaments: The Team Learning Approach.* Englewood Cliffs, N.J.: Educational Technology.

Dishon, D., and O'Leary, P. 1984. *A Guidebook for Cooperative Learning: A Technique for Creating More Effective Schools.* Holmes Beach, Fla.: Learning Publications.

Ellis, S., and Whalen, S. 1990. *Cooperative Learning: Getting Started.* Jefferson City, Mo.: Scholastic Professional Books.

Foyle, H. C. 1989. *Homework: A Practical Teacher's Guide.* Portland, Me.: J. Weston Walch.

_____ 1990. "Cooperative Learning and Creative Thinking." *Kansas ASCD Record* 8(4), 90-91. (ERIC Document Reproduction Service No. ED 332 969.)

_____ 1992. *Clinical Supervision: A Cooperative Learning Approach.* Emporia, Kan.: The Teachers College, Emporia State University Press.

Foyle, H. C., and Lyman, L. 1989. Cooperative Learning: Research and Practice. A paper presented at the Rocky Mountain Regional Conference for the Social Studies, Phoenix, Ariz. (ERIC Document Reproduction Service No. ED 308 131.)

Foyle, H. C., and Lyman, L. 1990. "The Cooperative Learning Environment: Restructuring Without Rebuilding." *ASCD Record,* 8 (3), 5–15, Kansas. (ERIC Document Reproduction Service No. ED 326 505.)

Foyle, H. C., and Lyman, L. 1991. "Cooperative Learning: What You Need to Know" A pamphlet for parents in the public education leaflet series. Washington, D.C.: National Education Association.

Foyle, H. C., and Lyman, L. 1993. *The Interactive Classroom: Cooperative Learning.* A videotape. Washington, D.C.: National Education Association.

Foyle, H. C., Lyman, L. R., and Morehead, M. A. 1989. "Cooperative Learning: Possible Solutions to Student and Teacher Problems." *Wisconsin Journal for Supervision and Curriculum Development* 14(1), 33–36.

Foyle, H. C., Lyman, L., Morehead, M. A., and Foyle, J. C. 1989. Interactive Learning: Creating an Environment for Cooperative Learning. A paper presented at the 44th Annual Conference of the Association for Supervision and Curriculum Development (ASCD), Orlando, Fla. (ERIC Document Reproduction Service No. ED 305 335.)

Foyle, H. C., and Perne, S. 1990. The Use of Homework and Cooperative Learning in an Elementary Classroom. A paper presented at the annual meeting of the Mid-Western Educational Research Association (MWERA), Chicago, Ill. (ERIC Document Reproduction Service No. ED 325-469.)

Foyle, H. C., Lyman, L., and S. A. Thies,. S.A. 1991. *Cooperative Learning in the Early Childhood Classroom.* Washington, D.C.: National Education Association.

Glasser, W. 1986. *Control Theory in the Classroom.* New York: Harper and Row.

———— 1992. *The Quality School: Managing Students Without Coercion.* New York: Harper and Row.

Graves, L. N., and Graves, T. *Cooperative Learning: The Magazine for Cooperation in Education.* Box 1582, Santa Cruz, Calif. 95061-1582.

Graves, T., and Graves, N. 1990. *A Part to Play: Tips, Techniques, and Tools for Learning Cooperatively.* Glen Waverley, Victoria, Australia: Latitude Media & Marketing.

Hertz-Lazarowitz, R., Sharan, S., and Shackar, C. 1981. "What Children Think About Small-Group Learning." In *Changing Schools: The Small Group Teaching Project in Israel,* Sharan, S., and Hertz-Lazarowitz, R. eds. Tel-Aviv University, Israel.

Johnson, D. W, and Johnson, R. T. 1987. *Learning Together and Alone.* Englewood Cliffs, NJ: Prentice-Hall.

_____ 1990. *Circles of Learning: Cooperation in the Classroom,* 3rd ed. Edina, Minn.: Interaction Book Company.

Joyce, B., Weil, M., and Showers, B. 1992. *Models of Teaching,* 4th ed. Englewood Cliffs, N.J.: Prentice-Hall.

Kagan, S. 1992. *Cooperative Learning.* San Juan Capistrano, Calif.: Resources for Teachers.

Kohn, A. 1986. *No Contest: The Case Against Competition.* Boston, Mass.: Houghton Mifflin.

Lyman, L. R. 1990. "Dealing with Misunderstanding in the Cooperative Classroom." *Kansas ASCD Record* 8(4), 1-3. (ERIC Document Reproduction Service No. ED 332 969.)

Lyman, L. R., and Foyle, H. C. 1988. "Cooperative Learning Strategies and Children." (ERIC DIGEST No. EDO-PS-88-5). ERIC, ED 306 003.

_____ 1990. "The Constitution in Action: A Cooperative Learning Approach." *Georgia Social Science Journal* 21(1), 24–34.

_____ 1990. *Cooperative Grouping for Interactive Learning: Students, Teachers, Administrators.* Washington, D.C.: National Education Association.

_____ 1991. "Teaching Geography Using Cooperative Learning." *Journal of Geography* 90(5), 223–26.

Male, M., Johnson, D. W., and Johnson, R. T. 1986. *Cooperative Learning and Computers: An Activity Guide for Teachers,* 3rd ed. Santa Cruz, Calif.: Educational Apple-cations.

Moorman, C., and Dishon, D. 1983. *Our Classroom: We Can Learn Together.* Englewood Cliffs, N.J.: Prentice-Hall.

Orlick, T. 1981. *The Second Cooperative Sports and Games Book.* New York: Pantheon Books.

Rhoades, J., and McCabe, M. 1985. *Simple Cooperation in the Classroom.* Willits, Calif.: ITA Publications.

Reid, J., Forrestal, P., and Cook, J. 1989. *Small Group Learning in the Classroom.* Portsmouth, N.H.: Heinemann.

Roy, P. A. 1990. *Cooperative Learning: Students Learning Together.* Richfield, Minn.: Patricia Roy.

Schmuck, R. A., and Schmuck, P. A. 1988. *Group Processes in the Classroom.* Dubuque, Iowa: Wm. C. Brown.

Sharan, Y., and Sharan, S. 1992. *Expanding Cooperative Learning Through Group Investigation.* New York: Teachers College Press.

Slavin, R. 1991. *Student Team Learning: A Practical Guide to Cooperative Learning,* 3rd ed. Washington, D.C.: National Education Association.

_____ 1990. *Cooperative Learning: Theory, Research, and Practice.* Englewood Cliffs, N.J.: Prentice-Hall.

Webb, N. 1985. "Student Interaction and Learning in Small Groups: A Research Summary." In *Learning to Cooperate, Cooperating to Learn,* Slavin, R. et al, eds. New York: Plenum.

Yates, B. C., and Foyle H. C. 1992. "Using Computers in the Social Studies Classroom: Consultation and Cooperative Learning." *Computers in the Social Studies: A Journal for Teachers* 1(1): 1, 3–4.

ACTIVITY SHEET APPENDIX

Activity Sheets: Chapter 2

FIGURE 2.1
ACTIVITY SHEET—SIGNATURE SCAVENGERS

1. _____ has a first name with more than six letters.
2. _____ has a last name with exactly five letters.
3. _____ has a first name that begins with a vowel.
4. _____ has a first name that has two or more syllables.
5. _____ has a long vowel sound in his/her first name.
6. _____ has a digraph *(ch-, wh-, sh-, st-)* in his/her name.
7. _____ has a first name with two or more of the same letter (Bill, Jennifer).
8. _____ has a first name with less than 6 letters.
9. _____ has a first name that ends in *y.*
10. _____ has a first name that has no letters that are written with "tails" below the line (Charles, Michelle).

FIGURE 2.2
ACTIVITY SHEET—INFORMATION

1. _____ has one or more brothers.
2. _____ has one or more sisters.
3. _____ has one or more dogs.
4. _____ has one or more cats.
5. _____ has a mother who works outside the home.
6. _____ has blue eyes.
7. _____ likes chocolate milk better than white milk.
8. _____ is eating the school lunch today.
9. _____ is wearing shoes with white laces.
10. _____ walked to school this morning.
11. _____ remembers what he/she had for dinner two nights ago.
12. _____ watched TV before school this morning.

FIGURE 2.3
ACTIVITY SHEET—CREATURE FEATURE

1. He let the _____ out of the bag.
2. She was as graceful as a _____ .
3. He's as stubborn as a _____.
4. He bought a _____ in a poke.
5. She took to her new class like a _____ to water.
6. I'll be there in two shakes of a _____'s tail.
7. The dinner guest ate like a _____.
8. Hey, man, don't have a _____.
9. An _____ never forgets.
10. A _____ can't change its spots.
11. The Stock Exchange can have a _____ market or a_____ market.
12. He was as crazy as a March _____.
13. The speaker had a _____ in her throat.
14. March went in like a _____ and came out like a_____.
15. It's raining _____s and _____s out there!
16. It's going to be so cold that it will be a three_____ night.
17. That person is as clumsy as a _____ in a china shop.
18. Hold your _____s! It will be your turn soon.
19. He eats so fast that he just _____s down his food.
20. The class really knew how to get the substitute's _____.
21. Muhammad Ali floated like a _____ and stung like a _____.
22. She wasn't really unhappy, she was crying _____ tears.
23. _____ see, _____ do.
24. Carl Sandburg said the fog comes in on little _____ feet.
25. What's sauce for the _____ is sauce for the _____.
26. That kid will be the _____ in the ointment on the field trip.
27. Go ahead! Are you _____?
28. See you later, _____!

FIGURE 2.4
ACTIVITY SHEET—MATCHING GAME

1. A food we like
2. Something we like to do
3. Something we like about school
4. A song we like
5. Something nice about our families

6. Something that we'd like to see more of in the world
7. Something we are wearing
8. Something we expect of a friend
9. A color we like
10. A television show we watch
11. A holiday we like
12. A person we admire

FIGURE 2.5
ACTIVITY SHEET — CLASSROOM POLL

How many brothers and sisters do you have?
0   1   2   3   4 or more

What is your favorite color?
Blue   Red   Green   Yellow   Another color

In what season were you born?
Spring   Summer   Fall   Winter

What is your favorite flavor of ice cream?
Vanilla   Chocolate   Strawberry   Chocolate Chip   Another flavor

What is your favorite subject in school?
Reading   Social Studies   Math   Science   Another subject

What is your favorite pet?
Dog   Cat   Fish   Bird   Another pet

What is your favorite holiday?
Halloween   Christmas   Thanksgiving
Fourth of July   Another holiday

What color are your eyes?
Blue   Brown   Green   Another color   Don't know

FIGURE 2.6
ACTIVITY SHEET—COMMUNICATION GROUP-BUILDER

1. Which students have good verbal skills?
2. Which students are leading or dominating their groups?
3. Which students are holding back from group participation?
4. Which students are not getting along?

129

5. Which students will need extra academic support from their groups in order to be successful?
6. Which students will need extra social support from their groups in order to be successful?
7. What social interaction skills seem to be strong in most of the groups?
8. What social interaction skills will need to be enhanced for these students to cooperate successfully together?
9. What concerns do groups or individuals have about working cooperatively?
10. Do students understand why they are working together cooperatively?

Activity Sheets: Chapter 3

FIGURE 3.1
ACTIVITY SHEET—STUDENT RIGHTS (1)

Group Members' Names:

Group Role
(Reader, Recorder, Encourager):

_____

_____

_____

_____

_____

_____

Directions: Select group roles and complete the information above. Next, discuss each of the following questions. After each member of your group gives ideas, take a group vote to decide if the group agrees or disagrees with the question. You must give at least one reason to support each answer you give.

1. Do students in this class have the right to say something that is not true about another student? If so, under what conditions?
2. Do students in this class have a right to use profanity (swear words)? If so, under what conditions?
3. Do students in this class have a right to have others listen politely to them while they are speaking? If so, under what conditions?
4. Do students in this class have a right to express an idea that most students don't agree with? If so, under what conditions?
5. How can we protect the rights we decided are important?

FIGURE 3.2
ACTIVITY SHEET—STUDENT RIGHTS (2)

Group Members' Names:

Group Role
(Reader, Recorder, Encourager):

_____

_____

_____

_____

_____

_____

Directions: Choose a different role than you had during Activity 1. Discuss each of the following questions. After each member of the group has given his or her ideas, take a group vote to decide if the group agrees or disagrees with the question. Give at least one reason to support each answer you give.

1. Does a student in this class have the right to leave his or her feet in the aisles? If so, under what conditions?
2. Does a student have the right to bring knives or other weapons to school? If so, under what conditions?
3. Does a student have the right to play games in which pushing, grabbing, or tripping other students takes place? If so, under what conditions?
4. Does a student have the right to talk, push, or run during a safety drill? If so, under what conditions?
5. How can we protect the rights we decided were important?

FIGURE 3.3
ACTIVITY SHEET—STUDENT RIGHTS (3)

Group Members' Names: Group Role
                               (Reader, Recorder, Encourager):

_____   _____

_____   _____

_____   _____

Directions: Choose a different role than you had during Activities 1 and 2. Discuss each of the following questions. After each member of the group has given his or her ideas, take a group vote to decide if the group agrees or disagrees with the question. You must give at least one reason to support each answer you give.

1. Does a student in this class have the right to take something that belongs to another student or adult in the room? If so, under what conditions?
2. Does a student have the right to copy answers from another student? If so, under what conditions?
3. Does a student have the right to bully students who are smaller or weaker than himself or herself? If so, under what conditions?
4. Does a student have the right to use textbooks, desks, and restrooms that are free of graffiti (marks, words, drawings that don't belong there)? If so, under what conditions?
5. How can we protect the rights we decided were important?

6. Are there additional rights, other than those we have discussed, that all members of our class should have? (The recorder should list any ideas that the group has determined.)

FIGURE 3.4
ACTIVITY SHEET—EVALUATION

Self-Evaluation for _____

I worked with _____ .

Directions: Circle "all," "some," or "not much" for each item.

1. I worked hard in my group *all, some, not much* of the time.
2. I listened to others *all, some, not much* of the time they were sharing ideas.
3. My group listened to me *all, some, not much* of the time that I shared ideas.
4. My group had good ideas *all, some, not much* of the time.
5. I enjoyed working with this group *all, some, not much* of the time.

Activity Sheets: Chapter 4

Figure 4.1
SAMPLE FEEDBACK SHEET

Skill _____

Group Members	Times Observed	What Was Said

FIGURE 4.2
ACTIVITY SHEET–TWO DOZEN

Directions: Find at least one correct answer for each set of numbers below. The numbers must equal two dozen (24). On line 9, choose another combination of four numbers between one and nine and provide a solution.

Set 1.	1	2	3	4
Set 2.	2	2	3	4
Set 3.	2	4	6	8
Set 4.	2	2	4	6
Set 5.	3	5	7	9
Set 6.	3	3	3	3
Set 7.	4	4	4	4
Set 8.	6	6	6	6
Set 9.	Your own problem and solution _____

FIGURE 4.3
ACTIVITY SHEET–THE COMMON SENSES

Sense	Things to Think of	Team Answers
SIGHT	Blue things Red things	
HEARING	Things that make a low sound Things that make a high sound	
SMELL	Things that smell good Things that have no odor	
TASTE	Sour things Sweet things	
TOUCH	Rough things Smooth things	

FIGURE 4.4
ACTIVITY SHEET—FAMOUS CONFLICTS

Directions: Who did not get along with:

1. The Three Little Pigs?
2. Snoopy?
3. Elmer Fudd?
4. Stephen Douglas?
5. The Capulets?
6. The Sharks?
7. Wile E. Coyote?
8. Captain Hook?
9. Aaron Burr?
10. Bobby Riggs?
11. The Hatfields?
12. Popeye?
13. The Sheriff of Nottingham?
14. Luke Skywalker?
15. David?
16. Al Capone?
17. The Klingons?
18. Montezuma?
19. Captain Ahab?
20. The tortoise?

FIGURE 4.5
ACTIVITY SHEET—COMMON TYPES OF CONFLICT

Types of Conflict	Examples
Sharing limited resources	Family members with one TV disagree about what program to watch.
	A student is accused of "hogging" the drinking fountain by classmates.
Sharing people	Two students want the teacher's help at the same time.
	A girl wants a classmate to be her exclusive "best friend."
Differing opinions or perceptions	Students disagree about who started the fight.
	Friends support different candidates in the student council election.
Perceived unkindness or unfairness	Students think the teacher has "pets."
	A boy is upset about the name he was called.
Differing personalities or customs	Students are reluctant to include a new student in their game. "He acts weird," they say.
	Students make fun of a student with a regional accent.
Safety or right/wrong	A student urges a friend to stand up in a rowboat.
	A student encourages another student to try an illegal drug.

FIGURE 4.6
ACTIVITY SHEET—CATEGORIZING CONFLICT

Instructions: Label each of the conflicts on this sheet as one of the following six conflict types.

Limited Resources	Opinions or Perceptions
Sharing People	Unfairness or Unkindness
Personalities/Customs	Safety/Right or Wrong

1. Students disagree about whether or not the runner was safe.

2. A boy wants his friend to play with his father's gun. "It's not loaded is it?"
3. Two siblings each want the last brownie at dinner.
4. Students tell jokes about a class member of a certain nationality, hurting that person's feelings.
5. Students all want to sit beside the student teacher on the class field trip.
6. A teenager wants his friends to ride with him when he drives home from a party where he has had too much to drink.
7. Students are resentful because their teacher promised them extra time at recess and changed her mind.
8. A group of girls tell a new group member that she must shoplift an item to join their club.
9. Students label a class member a "nerd" and try to keep her out of their group.
10. A kindergartner cries because he is the only boy in his class not invited to a birthday party.

Activity Sheets: Chapter 5

FIGURE 5.2
ACTIVITY SHEET—COLUMBUS MEMORY GAME

Columbus	Explorer who made four voyages to the New World
1492, 1493, 1498, 1502	Dates of Columbus' four voyages
Storms, Mutiny	Problems Columbus had on his four voyages
Sweet potato, Tobacco	Discoveries Columbus wrote about his voyage (1493)
Isabella, Ferdinand	Columbus got money for his first voyage from them.
Amerigo Vespucci	Explorer for whom America is named
San Salvador	Island where Columbus landed in 1492
India	The country Columbus thought the New World was in
1500	Number of men Columbus took on his second voyage
Nina, Pinta, Santa Maria	Ships Columbus used on his first voyage

FIGURE 5.3
ACTIVITY SHEET—GEOGRAPHY FIND

F I N D

Cities

States

Water

Nations

Activity Sheets: Chapter 6

FIGURE 6.1
ACTIVITY SHEET–ADVERTISING STRATEGIES

Directions: Advertisers use many techniques to get you to buy their products. Think of commercials or other advertisements in which you have seen the following strategies used.

1. *What a bargain!* The advertiser tells you that the product is inexpensive compared to other products. He or she may tell you how you can save money by using the product or how a special sale ("for a limited time only") makes the product a real value.

2. *Everybody has one!* The advertiser tries to convince you that the product is the"cool" or "in" thing to have. He or she may make fun of groups or people who don't use the product and portray people who do use the product as being very special.

3. *Stars use these!* Famous actors, sports stars, or cartoon characters advertise products. The advertiser hopes you will buy the product because you like or admire the celebrity. The famous person may or may not actually use the product.

4. *Lots of numbers!* The advertiser uses numbers to convince you that the product is reliable or inexpensive. Percentages are often used. You may need to do some math to tell whether or not the product is really a good value.

5. *Magical places!* The advertiser shows the product in an attractive or enjoyable setting. You then think about the product when you think of a fun and exciting place.

6. *Funny stuff!* The advertiser uses humor to catch your attention. Because the advertisement is funny, you may pay more attention to it and remember the advertised product.

7. *Save our world!* The advertiser tells you that the product is better for the environment than another product. He or she may tell you that if you buy the product, a part of what you spend will be donated to a worthy cause.

8. *Put downs!* The advertiser compares the product with one or more other products on the market. These ads are often unfair to the other product.

9. *Slogans!* Slogans are catchy words that are easy to remember (even if you don't want to). The advertiser will sometimes invent words to describe the product.

10. *Music!* Music is also used to draw attention to a commercial. A jingle is a slogan set to music that is easy to sing.

FIGURE 6.2
ACTIVITY SHEET—ADVERTISING ANALYSIS

Group Members: _____

_____

_____

_____

Reading Assignment: _____

_____

1. Why were the characters in your story advertising?
2. What product or service did they advertise?
3. What methods of advertising did they use?
4. Did the characters in the story use any of the strategies we discussed in class to advertise their product or service?
5. Did people buy the product or use the service in the story because of the advertisements?
6. How could the advertisements in your story have been improved? List three ideas as a group.

FIGURE 6.3
ACTIVITY SHEET—DETERMINING BEST VALUE

Products	Brand A			Brand B		
	Ozs.	Cost	Cost per Oz.	Ozs.	Cost	Cost per Oz.
Fresh carrots	16	$.39		32	$.68	
Bread	18	$.50		24	$.79	
Frozen pizza	8	$.89		16	$1.79	
Apple juice	32	$.89		64	$1.59	
Ketchup	28	$1.08		32	$1.28	
Hot dogs	12	$1.09		16	$1.39	
Lunch meat	12	$1.48		16	$1.88	
Toothpaste	4	$1.56		6	$1.99	
Cereal	13	$2.29		15	$2.88	
Cheese	24	$2.99		32	$3.89	

FIGURE 6.4
ACTIVITY SHEET—BEST VALUE SOFT DRINK

Directions: Complete the chart to find the best value.

Container	Ozs.	Total Ozs.	Cost	Cost per Oz.
Aluminum cans (12)	12 oz. per can		$2.89	
Glass bottles (6)	16 oz. per bottle		$1.89	
Plastic bottle (1)	2 liters		$1.15	

FIGURE 6.5
ACTIVITY SHEET—BONUS! FREE! PRIZES!

Group Members:

_____

_____

_____

1. Sometimes advertisers give bonus gifts or prizes when you buy their product. List some examples.
2. Why do you think advertisers give bonus gifts or prizes?
3. Have you ever bought something or asked your parents to buy something so you could get the bonus gift that came with it?
4. If you did, were you satisfied? Why or why not?

Figure 6.6
Activity Sheet—Control a Variable

(Whirlybirds)

Variable Material	Test 1	Test 2	Test 3	Average
Tissue Paper				
Typing Paper				
Oak-Tag Board				
Cereal-Box Cardboard				

Activity Sheets: Chapter 7

FIGURE 7.1
ACTIVITY SHEET—NATIONAL NAMES

Directions: Fill in the name of a country or region of the world to complete the items below.

Example: _____ Setter = Irish Setter

1. _____ meatballs	11. _____ goose
2. _____ shorts	12. _____ waffle
3. _____ nut	13. _____ ink
4. _____ checkers	14. _____ hat
5. _____ man-of-war	15. _____ treat
6. _____ toast	16. _____ sausage
7. _____ muffin	17. _____ cheese
8. _____ beetle	18. _____ goulash
9. _____ tape	19. _____ shepherd
10. _____ roulette	20. _____ flu

Can you think of other examples? If so, list them on the back of this paper.

FIGURE 7.2
ACTIVITY SHEET—SOME IMPORTANT PEOPLE

1. Susan B. Anthony. Advocate for women's rights. Arrested for voting in 1876. President of America's women's suffrage societies, 1892-1900.

2. Crispus Attucks. African-American. Killed in the Boston Massacre, 1770.

3. Elizabeth Blackwell. First female physician in America. Founded Women's Medical College in 1857.

4. Louis Brandeis. First Jewish Supreme Court Justice, 1916.

5. Ralph Bunche. African American winner of a 1950 Nobel Prize for efforts toward Middle East peace.

6. Rachel Carson. Wrote *Silent Spring,* 1962, focusing national concern on the environment.

7. Cesar Chavez. Founded the United Farm Workers' Union in California.

8. Charles Curtis. Native American from Kansas, Vice-President of U.S., 1929-1933.

9. Gertrude Ederle. First American woman to swim the English Channel, 1926.

10. Edward Gallaudet. Founded Gallaudet College, Washington, D.C., 1864, first college for the deaf.

11. Althea Gibson. First African-American tennis champion at Wimbledon and U.S. Singles, 1957.

12. S. I. Hayakawa. Asian-American interred in a detention camp during World War II. President of San Francisco State University and U.S. Senator from California.

13. Matthew Henson. African-American who placed U.S. flag at North Pole as part of Admiral Perry's expedition, 1909.

14. Theodor Herzl. Zionist Congress, 1897, led the first attempt to establish independent Jewish state in either Palestine or Uganda.

15. Oveta Culp Hobby. First secretary of Health, Education, and Welfare appointed by President Eisenhower, 1953.

16. Sybil Ludington. In 1777, at age 16, rode 40 miles to warn the militia that British troops were advancing. A native of the colony of Connecticut, her statue is in Carmel, New York.

17. Anna Mary Robertson Moses. Best American primitive painter. Painted from age 76 to 101.

18. Elizabeth Peabody. Established first kindergarten in U.S., 1860.

19. Frances Perkins. First woman to serve in U.S. Cabinet as Secretary of Labor under President Roosevelt, 1933.

20. Hiram Revels. First African-American U.S. Senator from Mississippi, 1870.

21. Benito Juarez. Full-blooded Native American, became President of Mexico, 1861.

22. Nellie T. Ross. First woman elected governor, Wyoming, 1924.

23. Grace Hopper. Major developer of COBOL computer languages and programmer of the UNIVAC computer. Admiral in U.S. Navy.

24. Samantha Smith. At age 11 wrote to Yuri Andropov, Soviet leader, pleading to stop nuclear arms race. Visited Russia in 1983. Died in airplane crash in 1985.

25. Jim Thorpe. Native American who won decathlon and pentathlon at 1902 Olympics.

26. Mae Jemison. First African-American female astronaut in space. As a physician, she joined NASA and flew on the space shuttle *Endeavour,* June, 1987. She left NASA in 1993.

27. Pancho Villa. Raided San Isabel, Texas, during the Mexican Revolution.

28. Emma Willard. Founded Troy Female Academy, the first women's college in U.S., 1821.

29. Andrew Young. First African-American U.S. ambassador to the United Nations, 1977. Mayor of Atlanta, 1982.

30. Ben Nighthorse Campbell. Native American Senator from Colorado, 1992.

Activity Sheets: Chapter 8

FIGURE 8.1
ACTIVITY SHEET—NUMBERS

Directions: Number these from smallest to largest amount.
1 = smallest amount.

The Seven Dwarfs + Snow White + the Prince

Value of the coin Abraham Lincoln is on

Number of things in a dozen

Number of wheels on two cars

Number of things in a pair

Number of kids in the Brady Bunch

Number of Teenage Mutant Ninja Turtles

Number of pins in bowling

Number of toes on one foot

Strikes a batter gets in baseball

FIGURE 8.2
ACTIVITY SHEET—GREAT

1. Name the five Great Lakes.
2. Name the countries that make up Great Britain.
3. Name a ruler with "great" in his or her name.
4. Name a type of dog with "great" in its name.
5. Name the period that occurred after the stock market crash of 1929.
6. Name the book by F. Scott Fitzgerald that has "Great" in the title.
7. Name Linus' hero in the *Peanuts* comic strip.
8. Name the U.S. President known as the "Great Communicator."
9. Name a bird with "great" in its name.
10. Write the math symbol for "greater than."

FIGURE 8.3
ACTIVITY SHEET—TEAM CATEGORY CHALLENGE

TEAM MEMBERS: _____

Letter	Description	Answer 1	Answer 2	Answer 3	Answer 4
A	Occupations (jobs) that begin with A				
B	Vegetables that begin with B				
C	Breeds of dogs that begin with C				
D	Names for money that begin with D				
E	Numbers less than 100 that begin with E				
F	Musical instruments that begin with F				
G	Plant-eating mammals that begin with G				
H	Buildings humans live in that begin with H				
I	Countries of the world that begin with I				
J	Presidents whose last names begin with J				
K	Animals of Australia and New Zealand that begin with K				
L	Parts of the human body that begin with L				
M	World capitals that begin with M				
N	Original 13 colonies that begin with N				
O	Colors that begin with O				
P	Sports actions that start with P				
Q	Verbs that begin with Q				
R	Artists whose names begin with R				
S	American cities that begin with S and have a major league baseball team				
T	Things that scare or bother people that begin with T				
U	U.S. state capitals that contain a U				
V	Models of cars that begin with V				
W	Sounds that begin with W				
X	Brand names that contain an X				
Y	Names of flowers that end in Y				
Z	Adjectives that contain a Z				

FIGURE 8.4
TEAM CATEGORY CHALLENGE—ANSWERS

Letter	Answers (other answers possible)
A	Actor, architect, artist, accountant, astronaut, attorney
B	Beets, broccoli, brussels sprouts, beans
C	Cairn terrier, collie, cocker spaniel, chow
D	Dime, dollar, deutsche mark, drachma, doubloon, dinar
E	Eight, eleven, eighteen, eighty-one
F	Flute, fiddle, fife, French horn, fluegelhorn
G	Goat, gopher, giraffe, groundhog, gazelle
H	House, hut, hotel, hogan, high-rise apartment, hospital
I	Iceland, Ireland, Iran, Iraq, Israel, India, Indonesia
J	T. Jefferson, A. Jackson, A. Johnson, L. Johnson
K	Kangaroo, kiwi, koala bear, kookaburra
L	Legs, lungs, liver, lips, lashes, lens
M	Madrid, Managua, Mexico City, Moscow, Manila, Monrovia
N	New Hampshire, New Jersey, New York, North Carolina
O	Orange, olive, orchid, ocher, oxblood
P	Pass, pitch, play, punt, putt
Q	Quash, quit, quiz, quip, quell, quiet
R	Raphael, Rembrandt, Remington, Renoir, Rivera
S	St. Louis, San Diego, San Francisco, Seattle
T	Tasmanian devil, tarantula, termite, thistle, typhoon, tick
U	Augusta, Austin, Baton Rouge, Columbia, Honolulu, Juneau
V	Volvo, Volkswagen, Vega, Volare, Ventura, Vanagon, Vauxhall
W	Whine, whisper, wail, wheeze, whistle
X	Borax, Rexall, Ajax, Exxon, Texaco, Xerox
Y	Daisy, lily, pansy, peony, poppy
Z	Crazy, dizzy, hazy, breezy, lazy

FIGURE 8.5
ACTIVITY SHEET—FALL COLORS

Red	Yellow	Brown	Orange

FIGURE 8.6
ACTIVITY SHEET—WHAT'S FOR LUNCH?

Directions: Below are lists of ingredients from familiar foods. Can you name the foods?

1. Cultured pasteurized grade A milk, skim milk, strawberries, sugar, corn sweeteners, nonfat milk solids, pectin, natural flavors, and lemon juice
2. Beef stock, tomatoes, potatoes, peas, green beans, corn, high fructose corn syrup, enriched alphabet macaroni, onions, celery, salt, potato starch, vegetable oil, yeast extract and hydrolyzed vegetable protein, monosodium glutamate, beef fat, dehydrated garlic, caramel color, natural flavoring, and oleoresin of paprika
3. Meat by-products, water sufficient for processing horsemeat, beef by-products, soy flour, salt, potassium chloride, guar gum, methionine hydroxy analouge calcium, DL-Alpha tocopheryl acetate (source of vitamin E), citric acid and ethoxyquin (preservatives), magnesium oxide, choline chloride, sodium nitrate (to promote color retention), iron carbonate, copper oxide, cobalt carbonate, vitamin A palmitate (stability improved), manganous oxide, zinc oxide, ethylenediamine dihydroiodide, thiamine mononitrate, D-Activated animal sterol (source of vitamin D-3), and vitamin B-12 supplement
4. Beef, water, dextrose, salt, corn syrup, spice, sodium erythorbate, flavorings, sodium nitrate, and oleoresin of paprika
5. Red ripe tomatoes, distilled vinegar, corn syrup, salt, onion powder, spice, natural flavoring
6. Sugar, gelatin, adipic acid (for tartness), disodium phosphate (controls acidity), fumaric acid (for tartness), artificial flavor, artificial color
7. Enriched wheat flour, malted barley flour, potassium bromate, sugar, eggs, vegetable shortening, salt, artificial vanilla flavoring, lecithin, baking soda, and a small piece of paper
8. Sugar, milk, cocoa butter, chocolate, soya lecithin (an emulsifier), and vanillin (an artificial flavoring)
9. Tomato juice from concentrate (water, tomato concentrate), reconstituted juices of carrots, celery, beets, parsley, lettuce, watercress, spinach, with salt, vitamin C (ascorbic acid), natural flavoring, and citric acid

Figure 9.3
ACTIVITY SHEET—SPRING

	Animals	Baseball Terms	Birds, Flowers	Green Things
S				
P				
R				
I				
N				
G				

Created by: Joanne Foyle, William Allen Elementary School, Emporia, Kansas

FIGURE 9.4
ACTIVITY SHEET—CATEGORIZING SOLUTIONS

CATEGORIES	POSSIBLE SOLUTIONS

Do something with the books.
1. Don't take books home.
2. Don't go home.
3. Buy an extra set of books for home.
4. Carry the books with me all the time (to dinner, when playing, when bowling).
5. Put the books near the clothes I will wear tomorrow.
6. Put the books in the car I will ride to school in tomorrow.

Place reminders on myself.
1. Tie a string around my finger.
2. Write a note on my arm before I go to bed.
3. Pin a note to my pajamas.

Place reminders elsewhere.
1. Put a note by the door.
2. Put a note on the refrigerator.
3. Put a note on the mirror.
4. Tie a string to my house key.

Ask others to remind me.
1. Ask my mom to remind me.
2. Have a friend call in the morning to remind me.
3. Ask my sister to remind me.

FIGURE 9.5
ACTIVITY SHEET—EXAGGERATION

Directions: Write an exaggerated sentence for each of the factual sentences below.

EXAMPLE:
(Factual Sentence)　　　The teacher gave us a lot of homework.
(Exaggerated Sentence)　She gave us so much homework it cost us three weeks allowance to buy enough pencils to do it.
　1. He was a fast runner.
　2. The meal at the restaurant wasn't very good.

3. She could figure out math problems quickly.
4. The teacher told boring stories about his childhood.
5. She made a good catch during the softball game.
6. He was a poor speller.
7. He could eat more than anyone in the class.
8. She wore too much make-up.
9. He could draw well.
10. He had trouble keeping his desk clean.

Activity Sheets: Chapter 10

Figure 10.1
Activity Sheet—Questions on *A Wrinkle in Time*

Instructions: Discuss the following questions in your group. All group members must be able to explain and give reasons for each answer. The group will write its answers and turn in one paper.

1. Why was Meg Murry having trouble in school?
2. What reasons can cause good students to do badly in school? (List at least three.)
3. If you were Meg's teacher, how could you help her?
4. If you were Meg's friend, how could you help her?

FIGURE 10.2
ACTIVITY SHEET—GROUP MEMBER ROLES FOR WORKING WITH LITERATURE

1. Storyteller—tells, writes, or tape records important information about the plot, main characters, ideas, and/or events of the story
2. Character Describer—describes major characters in the story
3. Actor—acts out part of the story
4. Reader—reads aloud part of the story
5. Mural Maker—creates a mural that depicts events in the story
6. Language Locator—locates examples of similes, metaphors, parts of speech, or other literary or grammatical devices in the story
7. Glossary Writer—locates difficult, unusual, or new words and writes definitions
8. Puppeteer—acts out parts of the story by using puppets
9. Editor—tells what parts of the story should have been left out or changed
10. Illustrator—draws or paints significant events or characters in the story
11. Advertiser—writes and performs a commercial encouraging others to read the story
12. Sequencer—writes major events of the story in order or creates a time line comparing story events to historical events
13. Mapper—draws a map and labels places mentioned in the story
14. Pre-fabricator—writes events that might have occurred before the

story took place
15. Re-finisher—writes another ending for the story
16. Builder—constructs a building, setting, or items mentioned in the story
17. Puzzler—creates crossword, acrostic, or other puzzles based on events, character names, or vocabulary words in the story
18. Performer—performs vocal or instrumental music or a dance related to the events in the story
19. Cover Designer—designs a book jacket with descriptive fly leaf about the book
20. Biographer—finds facts about the author of the story
21. Comparer—compares story events, characters, or setting to other stories
22. Futurist—predicts what might happen after the story ends or what characters in the book might be doing in five years
23. Economist—researches the cost of items used, trips taken, and other story-related expenses
24. Critic—writes a critical review of the story

Activity Sheets: Chapter 11

FIGURE 11.3
ACTIVITY SHEET—ADVERTISING PICTURE BOOK

Directions: Your group is to create and publish a picture book that demonstrates at least six advertising strategies commonly used by advertisers to sell their products. The materials used by your group in other advertising activities are one source of information for your book. Feel free to use any other resources that you can find to broaden your information. Accuracy of information, clarity in presenting your ideas to your audience, originality, creativity, risk taking, and quality of the finished product will all be used to evaluate your book.

Your book will be due _____(fill in the date).

You will be presenting your book to the class on _____ (fill in the date).

The rubric by which your book will be evaluated is the Rubric—Advertising Strategies (Figure 11.4).

FIGURE 11.5
ACTIVITY SHEET—JIGSAW COOPERATIVE LEARNING ASSIGNMENT

DAY 1:

By _____(date), each person will have read the assigned material.
Person 1:

Person 2:

Person 3:

Person 4:

Each person will prepare for a cooperative learning group by preparing a one-page listing of the title of the material read (or page numbers), source, and at least 10 important ideas from the material. This paper is used in the cooperative group, then turned in.

Each member of the group will meet with people from other groups (experts) who have read the same material in order to discuss the major ideas. These are the expert groups for covering this portion of the material. Each expert group will develop a list of the major ideas covered in the portion of material read by its members.

DAY 2:

Members will return to their cooperative group and all four members will teach their portion of the material to the other members of the group.

DAY 3:

The cooperative group will meet to review the information and prepare for the test. The individual quiz is then taken by each student.

The Authors

Lawrence Lyman is Professor in the Division of Educational Administration, The Teachers College, Emporia State University, Emporia, Kansas. He taught grades four through six and served as a principal at the elementary school level for 13 years.

Harvey C. Foyle is Associate Professor in the Division of Teacher Education, The Teachers College, Emporia State University, Emporia, Kansas. He taught in the public schools for 18 years.

Tara S. Azwell is Assistant Professor in the Division of Teacher Education, The Teachers College, Emporia State University, Emporia, Kansas. She taught at the elementary school level, grades one through five, for 20 years.

Lyman and Foyle have previously collaborated on two books published by the National Education Association: *Cooperative Grouping for Interactive Learning: Students, Teachers, and Administrators*, a book in the NEA School Restructuring Series, and *Cooperative Learning in the Early Childhood Classroom*, a book in the NEA Early Childhood Series (with Sandra Alexander Thies).

The Advisory Panel

David Bell, Professor of Education, Arkansas Tech University, Russellville, Arkansas

Geraldine Doswell, Guidance Counselor, Slackwood Elementary School, Lawrenceville, New Jersey

Faith Garrold, Supervisor of Instruction K–12, MSAD #3, Unity, Maine

Angie Gastall, Third Grade Teacher, Fall River Public School, Fall River, Massachusetts

Fannie P. Ott, K–3 Elementary Substitute Teacher, Ritzville, Washington